For Maya

Baltic Sea

EAST PRUSS

Königsberg

Danzig

GERMANY

POLAND

Vistula

WARSAW

Łódź

AUSCHWITZ

Moravská Ostrava

Cracow

Vistula

Bielsko-Biała

BESH MOUN'

Cieszyn

Těšín

CARPATI

SLOVAKIA

Kosice

VIENNA

MATRA MOUNTAINS

Bratislava

Nickelsdorf

Mosonmagyaróvár

AUSTRIA

100 Miles

160 Kilometres

BUDAPEST

HUNGARY

LITHUANIA

November 27, 1942 –
January 18, 1945

• Kaunas

Pripet   Marshes

Bug

BREST LITOVSK

Terespol •

odawa

Stawki

• Horodnice

• Lukov

Sobibor

• Vladimir Volynskij

Pripet

SOVIET UNION

VOLHYNIA

• Lvov

U K R A I N E

San

Latki

Kalina

Dniester

Jasna MOUNTAINS

RUMANIA

Introduction

I arrived in Göttingen for the session of the World Romany Congress. I checked into a small Central Hotel on Juden-strasse and walked through narrow winding streets to the Stadthalle, a modern three-storey Conference Centre, just on the outskirts of the old quarter of the German city. Upstairs, the big hall was filled by three hundred delegates from twenty-eight countries, who were listening to the brief speech of welcome by the President, Dr Jan Cibula. All the delegates' speeches were to be delayed until the next day for, as always with Gypsies, the first order of the conference was entertainment. While the Bhangra Dancers from India were making their way on to the stage to the accompani-ment of zithers, I looked around for the man who had invited me to the Congress, Grattan Puxon, the Secretary-General. He was sitting in the front row and as I elbowed my way towards him, we greeted each other. For the past year we had been corresponding, and my arrival in Göttingen was the result of that contact, which had begun when I decided to write a book about the Gypsy holocaust.

I returned to my hotel early, exhausted after my long journey, and was about to retire, when there was a knock on the door of my room and a bellboy brought me a letter. I opened the envelope, believing it would be an invitation to one of the many forthcoming functions. It read: "I am one of the Polish delegates to the Congress. I was told that you are planning to write a book about our wartime persecu-tion. It so happens that I have recorded many events in the

7

life of my family and my tribe during that period. I kept my notes in the hope that some day someone would want to use them, so that the world, especially America which can do so much for us, will know what we have gone through. I was told that you are an American writer of Polish origin, so you will easily be able to read what I have written. I am waiting in the hotel's lobby for your answer."

I walked downstairs. There, in the almost empty hall, I saw a lanky man in his mid-fifties, sitting alone at a small table, a glass of beer in front of him, holding a thick manila envelope. He stood up and extended his hand.

"I am Roman Mirga," he said. He pointed at the envelope. "This will tell you more than all the speeches you'll hear tomorrow, more than all the pamphlets and articles on the subject." I sat down and joined him in a glass of beer.

"Six million Jews were murdered by the Nazis," he continued, "but how many people know that 500,000 Gypsies perished at the same time? The Jews got individual and block compensation; we have received nothing, and discrimination against us continues all over the world. How can we hope to obtain any justice for our cause, to get funds, at least for the education of our children and grandchildren, the survivors of those who died, if the world does not know that they died?"

"I learned about it only a year ago," I said, defensively. "I promise you . . ."

"The Germans don't even admit that there was a Gypsy holocaust," he interrupted me. "There are memorials in Auschwitz for all the nations whose people died there, except for the Gypsies!"

"I promise you," I went on, "that I will read your material and meet you again tomorrow night."

The man grabbed my hand in both of his. "Thank you," he said. "I always wanted an American writer to write the book. What good would it do, if it were only published in Polish? Until now I have been unable to leave Poland and search for one. What a stroke of luck that you are American

8

and you are Polish, and that you are here." As I was reaching the staircase, he ran after me. "You must do it," he said, "so that I can keep the promise I made to my father. He was a great man, a great leader."

Next day I listened to the speeches of the delegates, their calls for the ending of prejudice, the supporting statements of Jews, such as that of the Nazi-hunter Simon Wiesenthal, and of many Christian sympathisers. I was surprised, however, that no representative of the German government, not even of a provincial government, was present at the Congress.

In the evening I opened the envelope. I was amazed by the writer's painstakingly detailed descriptions. It appeared that he had put down all his recollections shortly after the events had occurred. I began reading at six o'clock in the evening and became so absorbed by Roman Mirga's writing that I was unable to tear myself away. It had all the elements a writer needs – Gypsy lore, drama, characterisation. The evening session of the Congress was scheduled to begin at eight. I never went to it. I sat on my bed, reading, utterly fascinated, until I finished some time around ten. Half an hour later a bellboy called to say that a man was waiting for me downstairs.

There he was in the lobby, sitting at the same table as before, having a beer. He got up. "Have you read it?" he asked anxiously. He called the waiter. "Two more beers, please."

"You were right," I said enthusiastically. "It's all there, just as you said. When did you write it?"

"In 1944," the man answered. "On a Polish farm where I was hiding, in a cellar under the kitchen floor."

"Why don't you write it yourself?" I asked. "It could then be translated into English."

"I am not a writer. And I don't mind how it comes out, so long as it comes out in America, especially in America."

We drank our beers, then had two more. For several days afterwards I saw Roman Mirga a great deal. I made him fill

9

me in on all the details and add more of his recollections. After I left Göttingen I plunged into research on the subject, interviewing scores of eye-witnesses and delving into various archives in order to gather and to cross-check the information. It was Grattan Puxon, the Secretary-General and the founder of the World Romany Congress, and writers about Gypsy lore such as the British Dr Donald Kenrick and the Polish Jerzy Ficowski, who guided and assisted me. The Romany Congress officials in Bern and Salonica, those of Yad Vashem's Memorial Library in Jerusalem, and of the Association of Persecuted Peoples in Göttingen provided me with valuable background information. To all of them I am deeply indebted.

Then I started to write, allowing Roman Mirga to tell his own story and the stories of his family, his tribe, and of the forgotten holocaust of the Gypsy people.

PART ONE

1

I remember the date only too well, because on that day my entire life changed, shattered by events which were not of our own making. It was the evening of November 27, 1942. Our Gypsy trio was performing as usual at Fukier's Wine Cellar in Warsaw and the evening seemed to be no different from any previous ones. I was only seventeen at the time, but the details stand out in my mind as vividly as if it happened only yesterday.

My mother, a petite woman dressed in a long flowing colourful skirt, with strings of beads around her neck and copper bracelets on her wrists, was stepping briskly around the large room, shaking her tambourine as she sang in Polish, "From village to village/Gypsy girls are strolling/ They are strolling and telling fortunes . . ." Behind her were my father with his violin and myself with my accordion, providing the instrumental backing for the song and trying to drown the noise of raucous voices, the clatter of plates and the clinking of glasses which was accompanied by frequent shouts of 'Prosit!'

Outside, snow was falling and the cobbled main square of the Old Town was completely deserted; but inside the night club there was a holiday-like atmosphere as the German officers, and the high Polish officials who were collaborating with them, celebrated the early arrival of the winter.

We made our way slowly to the next room and then to a further one. The customers at the candlelit tables threw coins to the Gypsy band, which was playing while they enjoyed their sausages with sauerkraut and drank glasses of vodka, served by waitresses in white dresses with red aprons – the Polish national colours.

When the song ended we returned to the main room and sat down on stools in the corner between two huge casks of wine. "What time is it?" I asked.

My father pulled his golden watch out from his waistcoat pocket and snapped open its cover. "Almost midnight. Two more hours." He patted me on the knee. "You'll be getting your own watch for Christmas – and for your birthday, Roman." Christmas Day was also my birthday. I felt my father proudly scanning first my suit, its green jacket with shining golden buttons identical to his own, and then my unGypsylike face with its thin lips, blond hair, small nose and blue eyes.

I grinned. "A pocket one, like yours?"

"Like mine, son."

I drew a deep breath, then turned back to the room where a very young waitress, with long flaxen braids, was serving a perspiring Pole as he kissed his lady friend's fingertips. My mother chuckled. "Our boy is certainly growing up," she said, addressing her husband. Amongst ourselves we always spoke Polish.

A bald, well-fed-looking man came over, snapping his fingers. "Dymitr, keep on playing," he said to my father. "The customers are calling for more music."

" 'When a Gypsy makes his violin cry'," my mother suggested, adjusting her green waistcoat over her slender but full figure.

My father nodded. He tossed back his black hair, then tucked his violin under his chin. I picked up my accordion from the floor, but waited, for the first part of the number was a violin solo. I watched my father as he played alone on the podium, his fine manly figure straight as a ramrod. Then he stepped down, which was the signal for my mother and me to join him. We began moving around, stopping at each table, making each customer feel that we

14

were playing the lilting, romantic tune exclusively for him. The room was filled with cigarette smoke and permeated by the mingled odours of cheap perfume, sauerkraut and alcohol. As we came to a group of black-uniformed SS officers with twin silver flashes on their collars, one of them, a good-looking and broad-shouldered lieutenant, suddenly hit his fist against the table, overturning his half-filled glass. A waitress rushed to wipe up the drink. "Zigeuner!" the German shouted, wagging his finger. "Stop playing your phoney tunes!" I looked up at my father and saw him halt his bow, as his long, narrow eyes under their bushy brows blinked nervously. We all understood German. Gypsies pick up languages quickly.

The officer got up, propping himself against the table. Only now did I notice two plump women in the officers' company, one of whom, with a bosom bulging almost out of her blouse, was sitting next to the lieutenant. There was no doubt that he was trying to impress her. "You can fool all these people," the German went on, "but not me, Zigeuner! I know what real Gypsy music is. Play that, or don't play at all!"

The night club manager appeared, his forehead covered with beads of sweat. "I'm sorry, sir," he said, before snapping his fingers at my father. "Play," he ordered in broken German, "what the officer is asking for."

I looked at the lieutenant. He was dark-haired, with a swarthy complexion and an odd triangular cleft between his white upper teeth. I smiled inwardly, for the man did not look at all like a member of the Aryan race, but more like a Gypsy. My eyes darted to my father. With a sigh he tucked his violin back under his chin. Then he struck the opening chords of Brahms' Hungarian Dance. My mother began to dance around the room, banging on her tambourine, her eyes anxiously fixed on the German officer. Uncertainly, I joined in with my accordion. The officer's face broke into a self-satisfied smile. He sat back and put his arm around the Polish woman. "That's it," he said

15

archly. "This is real Gypsy music." Then he became tipsily intellectual. "You see," he went on, speaking to his female companion, "Brahms, Liszt, *they* composed the real Gypsy music. Hundreds of others merely tried to imitate them. What they have been playing up till now is phoney, it is not even composed by Gypsies. It doesn't matter that Brahms and Liszt were not Gypsies either, but they did thorough research. You know what research is, Liebchen?" The lieutenant picked up a bottle and filled the girl's glass and his own, then downed his drink at a gulp. The woman shook her head; she did not understand what the lieutenant was talking about, but the German, undaunted, went on. "I am a doctor, you see? A physician, but also a scientist. I love medical research. Music is like medicine. To practise it correctly also requires research. Besides, I am connoisseur of music, they can't fool *me*!"

The girl gave the German an admiring peck on his cheek. "A doctor, eh?" she said, flattered.

We played the tune through and, when we finished, the officer got up and clapped, shouting, "Bravo! Bravo!" All the others in the room, and even the adjacennt rooms, took the hint and added their applause to his. "Now, Liszt!" the lieutenant ordered. "Here, Zigeuner, have some schnaps."

He filled a glass with vodka and handed it to my father. "And you, too." He poured another one for me. My father drained his glass. His forehead furrowed as he watched me unable to refuse my first-ever alcoholic drink. I barely touched my glass and put it down, but the German lieutenant would have none of that. "You are a man, aren't you?" he said. Much as I hated the taste, and the German hovering over me, I had to finish my drink. "Now, Liszt!"

My father gave us a nod and started one of Liszt's rhapsodies, all the time standing by the officer's table. When we finished, the lieutenant led the entire audience in loud applause. The club's manager rushed to him. "Gut?" he asked.

16

"Sehr gut," the lieutenant answered. He dug into his pocket and slipped a few banknotes into my father's hand.

"Thank you, sir." My father was about to move away when the officer beckoned to him.

"Wait! Here!" He pulled out a visiting card and handed it to my father. "This is a civilian card. I'm on leave here from the front, near Moscow. Soon we'll reach there and the war will be over. Come to my town, will you? Gunzburg in Bavaria. I can obtain a long and lucrative engagement for you there. Our family practically owns Gunzburg. Mengele," he said. "The family name is Mengele. Farm machinery. Karl Mengele und Söhne."

I glanced at the card in my father's hand. "Dr Josef Mengele," it read. "M.D., Ph.D." We would never go to Bavaria, I thought. What for? My parents had played at Fukier's Wine Cellar for several years now and I had joined them when I was barely thirteen. We performed first for the Poles, then for the Germans. The sentimental Poles loved and appreciated our music. But, as if answering my doubts about the Germans, Lieutenant Mengele said, "I am a romantic at heart; and I love Gypsies. We have them in Gunzburg too. But not one of them plays as well as you." He grabbed my father's elbow. "Go on, play some more, Zigeuner!" He slipped a few more banknotes into his hand and looked at the buxom blonde for approval of his largesse. My father motioned to us to take a rest. He would play a solo. From my stool I watched him as he smoothed his moustache, happy with the large tip he had received; then he raised his violin and began to play.

Again Janka, the young waitress, attracted my attention as she passed by, smiling at me, striding easily and gracefully, balancing her tray with a bottle and glasses high over her head. I felt the stubble on my face and stuck my chin out jauntily. It was high time I started shaving, I decided. And I would grow a small moustache. I hunched my shoulders in anticipation. The alcohol was going to my head. I felt I had the courage to do what I had wanted to do

17

for so long – to ask Janka for a date, to take her to the Luna Park, or the skating rink in Saxony Gardens, or even to a cinema. A spasm hit me in the pit of my stomach. Strange, but pleasant. Yes, I felt I was growing up, and becoming a man – just like my father.

We left the night club as usual at two in the morning, leaving a few drunk customers behind, refusing to go. Snow was still falling, covering the cobblestone square and the roofs of three-storey medieval houses surrounding it. "He was very generous, that lieutenant," my father said. "Two hundred zlotys! You can buy fifteen loaves of bread with that."

"Or a dress," my mother said. "For Mara. Your daughter needs a new dress for Sundays."

"But she has dresses. Nice ones."

"They don't fit her any more. You forget how fast nine-year-old girls grow."

My father gave a magnanimous wave of his hand. "Oh, all right, Wala. A watch for the boy, a dress for the girl."

We were leaving the Old Town, crossing the wide avenue, tram-rails down the middle, with no one in sight and darkened windows gazing at us like blind eyes. As we approached the Vistula River, we saw some men in uniform emerging from the direction of the Presidential Palace where President Mościcki used to live before the war. "Hey!" They were Polish voices and we were relieved that they were not German ones. "Stop!" We halted.

The three Blues, so nicknamed because of the colour of their uniforms, approached us. "Your Kennkarten!" one of the three policemen said. We went through that ritual almost every night on our way home. "Here," my father said. He carried not only his own but also my mother's and my identity cards. One of the Blues read them. "Gypsies, eh?" he said, then added, "Ausweise!" My father showed him the three certificates showing our names, our place of employment and our right to be on the street during

18

curfew. "Ah, at Fukier's Wine Cellar?" the man said. "Good, you may go. You live in the Praga?"

"Yes."

"You don't happen to have a bottle of wine or some cigarettes? We'll buy them from you."

"No, I don't drink and don't smoke."

"Just play the fiddle and tell fortunes, eh?" He handed my father back the documents.

We walked on. We crossed the Kierbedzia Bridge, our footsteps making a crunching sound on the snow, our eyes curiously watching the thin patina of ice which in some places covered the river. On the left bank of the Vistula there was the Praga, the largest suburb of Warsaw. We walked by the Luna Park, with its Ferris wheel visible over its tall evergreen hedge, past the Praga cinema and a small neglected park, then turned into a side street. We lived a bare fifteen minutes' walk from our place of work, and soon we reached Panienska Street, tired and glad to be home.

We mounted the dark staircase to the third floor and stopped in front of the door with the name plate 'Dymitr Mirga, musician'. My father pulled out his key. We entered the room as quietly as we could, anxious not to awake my sister. We were surprised by the wan yellow light of a smoky acetylene lamp hanging on the wall, not visible from outside because of the curtained window. On the edge of her bed in the living room sat Mara, in her long nightdress, pretty with dark, beribboned braids and a dark complexion. She did not look like me, but like all little Gypsy girls.

"Why are you up?" my father asked. My sister turned her head and pointed her chin at the kitchen. "Who is there?" my father whispered with alarm.

At the sound of his voice, the kitchen door creaked open and there appeared a burly, dishevelled man, about forty, his clothes torn, streaks of blood caked on his face. "My God!" my mother exclaimed. "Danko! Danko Mular!"

19

It was my father's cousin, and he fell straight into his arms. "I escaped from the ghetto!" he gasped, speaking in the Romany dialect of the Lowland Gypsies. "We broke out of the Gęsia Street Prison." He embraced me, then my mother.

"Ghetto? What were you doing in the ghetto?" my father asked.

"Sit down, Danko," my mother said. "Let me clean your face. Mara, bring a basin of water and a towel."

"We fought the prison guards and killed two of them." Danko raised his arms. "With these!" he said, his haggard, angular dark face expressing both anger and pride. Then he sank into a chair as Mara returned from the kitchen. She handed the towel to my mother who started to bathe Danko's face. "We broke out of the prison, climbed the wall, the ghetto wall, then split, all ten of us. I made my way to you by dashing from courtyard to courtyard or hiding in the dark shadows of walls. The curfew helped."

My father sat heavily opposite his cousin. "Lucky you remembered the way. It's over three years since you were last here."

"In the summer of 1939," Danko said, "just before the war. On my way to Łódź to join a band." He flinched as my mother pulled his hair aside to attend to the wounds on his scalp.

"Why did they send you to prison? What did you do? Did they take you for a Jew?" my father asked, bewildered.

"What did I do? I was born a Gypsy, that's what I did. You mean – you don't know what's happening to us! No, they did not take me for a Jew. But now they are treating us the same way. Don't you keep in touch with other Gypsies?"

"Not lately," my father answered. "We work late, sleep late, the children go to school . . . And there aren't any Gypsy bands in Warsaw except ours."

"You have turned away from us, Dymitr," Danko said sadly. "You are a forytka Roma, a town Gypsy. So have I

20

been these past three years – but I haven't lost contact with my people."

"We were in Brest Litovsk a year ago," my father said defensively. "In our tribe's winter camp. We saw my parents, your parents. They all felt safe. The Jews were in the Brest Litovsk ghetto, but nobody was molesting the Gypsies."

"Three months ago Himmler issued an order – to deal with us," Danko went on. "There are plenty of Gypsies in the Warsaw ghetto. Whole families. They are all wearing the 'Z' sign for 'Zigeuner' instead of 'J' for 'Jude'." He flinched again as my mother cleaned his face, peeling off the bloody, dirty scab.

"Get me the iodine," she said to Mara.

"You must be wondering," Danko said, "what I am doing in Warsaw? I escaped from the Łódź ghetto. That was the only ghetto with Gypsies in it as well as Jews. The Nazis wanted to get rid of their Gypsies, so they sent five thousand Sinti there from Germany. Then they added those arrested in the town. My being a violinist did not stop them. Your turn will come too, even though you may feel safe for a time. I wasn't in any important night club. They keep you at Fukier's because it's *their* club, for their amusement, I suppose, but you won't escape in the long run. Even if you speak Polish at home and send your children to a Polish school." He gasped as my mother put iodine on his injuries.

I felt a cold running through my veins. I looked at my father for a reassuring word that we were safe, that nothing would happen *to us*. My father's Adam's apple twitched and drops of sweat came out on his forehead. "You must be hungry," my mother said to Danko.

"Hungry! All we had in prison was watery soup and a chunk of stale bread – once a day!"

"I'll warm some soup for you. Thick barley soup." She left for the kitchen. We heard the hiss of the primus stove, then my mother returned with some potatoes and a glass

21

of sour milk. "Eat this meanwhile." I watched my cousin devour the food like an animal. He drank the glass of milk in two huge gulps.

"Why did they put you in prison?" my father asked.

"They caught me when I reached Warsaw. At the railway station. I fought, resisted the arrest, that's why. Dymitr, for God's sake, wake up! You must run. Listen to me. Take your family and run! Hide in some forest."

My father's troubled eyes travelled to my mother, then to me and my sister. Little Mara began to cry softly. My mother brought Danko his soup, then went over to my sister and put her arm around her. "Nothing will happen to us, Mara," she said. "Right, Dymitr?" Her voice broke a little as she, too, looked at her husband for comfort.

Father tightened his mouth. The dimple in his chin became more pronounced. But he kept silent, waiting for Danko to finish his soup and carry on with his story.

I shook my head, bewildered, trying to understand what was happening. Jews, yes, I knew all about the Jews and their ghetto. The Wall was not far from Fukier's, on Miodowa Street. But why Gypsies? And why us? We had lived in Warsaw for ten years. My father was a marvellous violinist. Very few Gypsies could play Brahms or Liszt. The Germans needed us. Their Polish night club manager had good connections; he even knew Gunther Sauer, the Gestapo chief of Warsaw, who came to Fukier's at least once a week. I waited for my father to shake off his gloom and suggest some way out of the situation. He finally noticed the pleading in my face and straightened in his chair. "Let me hear everything, Danko," he said.

Danko finished his soup, then wiped his mouth with the sleeve of his jacket.

"In the Łódź ghetto I saw hundreds of our people die of typhus. Then the Germans started to transport the healthy ones. They said, for resettlement in the East. The East turned out to be Chelmno, a concentration camp in the north. Perhaps they were being killed there, I thought, so

I ran away. In the Warsaw ghetto, in August, they started to round up Jews by the thousands, also for resettlement in the East. The East this time was east, Treblinka, also a concentration camp. And, I believe, also death. They don't treat us differently any longer, Dymitr. They say – not for racial reasons as we are originally from India – we *are* Aryans. But they say for social reasons – we are nomads – thieves, criminals and parasites." He closed his eyes for a moment, exhausted by all that had happened to him. "I need to sleep," he said. "Please, cousin. Tomorrow I must go to Anin. We all – those who escaped – agreed to meet in the Anin Forest."

My father gulped hard, then after a pause, said, "And you want us to come with you?"

"No," Danko said. "We swore among ourselves that, if we managed to escape, we would all meet and form a Gypsy partisan group to fight the Nazis. But you, Dymitr, it's different for you. You have a family, women."

"I also have parents," Father said. "I must think of them. And Wala's parents. And the others – my relatives, my kumpania."

"You left them," Danko said, "years ago."

"I never did," Father answered, "not in my heart. Wala, let him sleep in Mara's bed and Mara can sleep with us. During the night I will think about what to do and in the morning I'll let you know what I decide." He looked at me, saw my concern, and gave me a smile. "Don't worry, son," he said. "Your father will think of something."

"Yes," Mother said to my sister, "your father will think of something. As always. Come to bed now."

I lay in bed in my room unable to sleep. In my mind's eye I saw images of Warsaw, the town I grew up in, my friends in school, the soccer stadium where I often played on summer afternoons, the nearby forest of Anin where my family and I used to go for picnics and where Danko now planned to form his band of partisans. I thought of the parks and palaces and beautiful churches, the music of their bells reverberating through the streets on Sundays when, dressed in our best, we went to Mass. Yes, we were more than forytka Roma, town Gypsies, we were bareforytka Roma – big-town Gypsies, no doubt resented and envied by our own kumpania. But this was what my father had wanted, for his children even more than for himself – a nice apartment, good and secure jobs, a decent education. Next June I would finish high school. How many Gypsies were given that opportunity? I found myself suddenly very calm, certain that my father would find some way of remaining in Warsaw. The manager of our night club would certainly help; he needed us. How many times hadn't the German customers expressed their joy at passing an evening in such an atmosphere, the Gypsy music allowing them to forget the war? And the manager knew the Gestapo chief. If there was any danger to us personally, would Sturmbannführer Gunther Sauer not tell the manager and the manager tell us?

I heard my parents' voices from their bedroom, quiet and calm, but I could not make out the words. Tiredness overtook me and I fell into a deep, restful, confident sleep.

I was awakened by the daylight and heard my father pulling aside the curtains of the window. "It's seven o'clock," I heard him say. "Come, we must fetch our instruments. There is a charwoman at the club now. We can go and get them."

"What for?" I asked, yawning, closing my eyes and turning back to the wall. "Do you want to practise a new number? Will I get to school on time?"

"You are not going to school," my father replied. "We are leaving. We are going away, but not to the forest. We are going to our camp in Brest Litovsk, to get your grandparents and all the others and then travel south to Hungary before it's too late."

I abruptly sat up in bed. The snoring from the living room reminded me that Danko was there. The recollection of what had happened to him and other Gypsies instantly sobered me.

"There are no Germans in Hungary and plenty of opportunities for us," my father said. "Come on, get up, son. We mustn't waste any time."

Wearing our overcoats and hats, my father and I walked quickly over the snow-packed pavement. Still groggy from sleep, I glanced at him again and again, waiting for him to speak, to reveal his plans further, but not daring to ask any questions.

We crossed the Cracow Suburb Boulevard, stopping for a moment to let the number 21 tram pass, its first car bearing a sign 'Nur für Deutsche'. The street was alive with the shouts of newsboys, "New Courier! Big losses inflicted on the Russians at Stalingrad!" No word about last night's break-out at the Gęsia Street Prison. At the entrance to the Old Town there was a small bazaar, with shabbily dressed people selling trinkets, old clothes and tin cans from their pushcarts, while boys in peaked caps peddled cigarettes at thirty zlotys a pack. As we approached Fukier's Wine Cellar, a droshky went by, carrying a German officer on leave from the Russian front who was cuddling his girlfriend as she showed him the sights of the city. My father led the way into the night club through a side entrance. The charwoman replied to our greeting and, unconcerned, continued with her chore of mopping the floor. We picked up our instruments from a cupboard in the rear room of Fukier's.

Back on the street, I slung the heavy accordion over my shoulder by its strap, my hand holding its base to ease the weight. "Tonight," I spoke for the first time since we left home, "when we don't turn up for work, they will know that we've left."

"By that time we will already be in our camp."

Strange, I reflected, for my father to use that expression 'our camp'. In the past he had always referred to the place

25

as our grandparents' camp. I never liked going there, even for a brief Christmas holiday. I had nothing in common with my people or their custom of wandering all over the country; only in winter did they settle in their wagons on the banks of the Bug River, at the same place year after year.

A procession of girls wearing coats and long white stockings passed us by, accompanied by two nuns. "What time does our train leave?" I asked.

"Half past eleven," my father answered. "I bought the tickets this morning." The Eastern Station was only ten minutes' walk from our home.

When we reached the apartment, Mother was busy packing our valises, my sister helping her. Danko was sitting at the table, drinking chicory. He had just woken up. "Wala told me," he said to my father. "You're doing the right thing. But going by train is dangerous. She told me you have permits from last year. Are they still valid?"

"I checked them. They are valid until the end of this year. But only to Brest Litovsk and back. How do you feel this morning?"

"Rested. I'll be going soon."

"How will you get there?"

"On foot. Or perhaps I'll get a lift from some peasant. It's less than twenty kilometres away."

"Your clothes are all torn. Here!" Father pulled a suit out of his wardrobe. "Put this on."

"A real gentleman's suit!" Danko changed quickly, then looked at himself in a mirror hanging on the wall. "Do I look like a gadje?" he asked with a chuckle.

"No," my father said soberly. "You'll never look like a non-Gypsy. No clothes will ever alter your face or your hair, so be careful!"

"Oh, I will be, don't you worry. They won't catch me," the man who had been caught twice said confidently. "Make sure you destroy everything that could lead them to Brest Litovsk."

"They won't find out," Father answered. "One good thing about the Gypsies – no written language, no letters to burn."

"How about Fukier's manager? Doesn't he know you are from Brest Litovsk?"

"No. He never asked, and I never told him."

Mother came out of the kitchen with a paper bag filled. "Here," she said, handing it to Danko, "some food for the road."

"Thank you." Danko embraced my mother, kissed Mara on her forehead, then shook hands with my father and me. "You know," he said, "it's the first time we Gypsies have fought the Germans. And I was one of those who did. I myself strangled one of the two men we killed." His swarthy face was exultant. "Explain to my parents that I had to stay behind and kill more of them. Look!" He dug a hand into his pocket and pulled out a revolver. "I wrested it off a Nazi officer. And that's how we plan to get our arms. From the enemy. God knows if and when and where we shall see each other again, but please tell them in the camp, Dymitr, tell them – Danko is fighting the Nazis."

"I will tell them."

My father walked his cousin to the door and waited until Danko had disappeared at the bottom of the staircase. Then he returned and started to help my mother pack. By half past ten we were ready. Mother looked sadly around the living room of our apartment. I saw her sigh deeply. "This has been our home for so many years," she said. "And we have to leave so much behind." She began to weep. "Our porcelain, the carpet I bought on the Kiercelak market, the icebox and the radio – they all took us months and months to save for."

"Please," Father said, "don't cry. You know I can't bear you to cry."

Mother quickly wiped her tears away, but then she saw Mara's face desperate with misery. "My dolls," my sister said in a hollow strangled voice. "They will feel so lonely in the empty house."

27

"Take one with you," my father said impatiently. "And stop crying! We must go now."

Mara picked up Mirka with her ragged dress and broken back, the first doll she ever received from her parents. We left, carrying our valises and the musical instruments, and walked to the main street, stopping now and again to rest. When we were about to turn at the street corner, Mother halted, taking a final look at the windows of our house. I forced myself not to look, and with all the strength I could muster held back the tears that were welling up in my eyes. My father hailed a droshky, which was being driven by a large man wearing an overcoat and a fur hat with raised earflaps. "Eastern Station," Father said. One after another he and I lifted our valises which the man stacked next to himself on the front seat. We bundled ourselves into the back of the carriage with our instruments. The driver smacked his lips to urge his horse forward.

As we drove to the station, we all looked out – at the newsboys jumping in and out of the trams, at the women with their shopping nets waiting in long queues in front of butcher shops and bakeries, at the droshkies rolling by with young couples unaware of the war and only conscious of each other, and the snow prettily covering the streets and roofs. A truckful of armed storm-troopers, with death's-heads on their caps and collars, roared by. The droshky detoured around a flower-bed, which in late November had no flowers, and halted in front of the station building carrying a bi-lingual sign, 'Ostbahn – Eastern Station'.

The driver handed down our suitcases. As Father was paying the fare and getting change, I watched three young German soldiers who were having their pictures taken by a street photographer against a painted canvas of the Belvedere Palace and the sign 'Gruss aus Warshau'. Dragging our valises, we made our way through the station hall right on to platform No.1, where our train was waiting, filled with peasants going home after selling their farm produce in the big city. The station was loud with the chuffing and snorting of engines together with the clanking and banging of wagons being shunted. My father led us to a carriage, scanning the compartments from the corridor until he found a half-empty one. He motioned to us and finally we were all seated in our places, after putting our valises and instruments up on the luggage racks.

A quarter of an hour or so later a red-capped station master appeared and blew his whistle to signal the train's departure. With a nostalgic wail, the locomotive began its journey, the wheels picking up speed as the train moved out of the station past the tall brick buildings of the Praga suburb.

I looked out of the window. I put my arm around my little sister who was holding her ragged doll. The tears finally had to come; my eyes glistened as I said farewell to my home-town, my friends, my unfinished education, my carefree youth, and our so hard-won and so easily lost way of life that I might never know again.

2

The sun was setting as we left the train at Brest Litovsk station. My mother carried Mara in her arms, sound asleep after the ordeal of the past night and the long train journey. My father and I dragged the valises and the instruments. We crossed the huge hall, past the first-class restaurant which was filled with German soldiers and the second-class one where drunken Poles were trying to forget the war by drinking home-distilled vodka.

Outside, rows of droshkies awaited the incoming passengers. There were no sleighs yet, for the snow that had fallen did not herald winter. We waited for our turn and then got into a carriage, with our valises and instruments piled up in front. "Where to?" the coachman asked. He had a huge walrus moustache and red glistening eyes, and I was sure he had been killing time waiting for customers with occasional sips of alcohol from a bottle kept under his seat.

"The Gypsy camp," my father said.

The driver turned and took a long look at his customers. We were dressed no different from others, but the man scrutinised our faces, dark and swarthy, except for mine. "You are Gypsies?" he asked matter-of-factly, without any hostility.

"Yes," Father said. "Is the winter camp still there, on the bank of the Bug?"

"Of course," the driver said. "Viooo!" He smacked his lips and tugged at the reins. His horse moved on.

"How are the Germans behaving here?" my father asked

as the droshky moved slowly over the railway bridge. "Are they making trouble – I mean for us Gypsies?"

"No," the man answered. "Jews yes, Gypsies no. There are no more Jews in Brest Litovsk."

I saw my father breathe a sigh of relief, but then he turned pale. "What do you mean? They used to live in the ghetto."

"There is no more ghetto," the driver said, then again he smacked his lips with a 'Viooo!' sound. We were travelling fast down The Union of Lublin Street. "A month ago, in a single day's operation, they evacuated it. They said 'evacuation'. We all know what that means."

My father rubbed his face. Out of some 70,000 inhabitants of Brest Litovsk 40,000 had been Jews. "What does it mean?" he asked, anxiously.

"Camps. Concentration camps. Possibly death. Poor people. But you Gypsies, you have nothing to worry about, you are not Jews."

Some people, I reflected, are, at least in German eyes, worse than the Gypsies. Some consolation!

We fell silent, as the deepening twilight penetrated the street, shrouding St Joseph's Catholic Church, the sports stadium, the ice-skating rink and the two-storey houses of the Polish inhabitants of the town. At the corner of Jagello Street, where Liberty Park stretched away into the country, the carriage turned along the park's wooded area away from Brest Litovsk towards Twierdza – the Fortress – where an entire Polish division used to be stationed before the Red Army took it over, only to be ousted from it by German Panzers. Some two kilometres out of Brest Litovsk, just before reaching the barracks of the Fortress, the droshky turned left along a wooded path, leading towards the Bug River. By now it was dark and the first stars and a bright moon illuminated the sky. I saw my father craning his neck with great eagerness. And then suddenly he saw it, we all saw it. In a large clearing in the woods, right over the river bank, there were dozens of open fires, lighting up the big

31

wooden wagons and a few tents. Between the trees stood the canvas-covered carts used for travelling. The familiar sounds of voices, tuning of instruments and the braying of horses made my father break into a big smile. "We are home," he said. He noticed my dubious expression and patted me on my knee as was his habit. "Jamaro kher," he said in Romany. "Our home. Home is where you are brought up and where your parents live."

I bit my lips, but said nothing of what I was thinking – of the kher on the third floor of Panienska Street in the Praga suburb of Warsaw where I had been brought up and where my parents used to live.

"You forget," my mother said to her husband. "We didn't come here to stay, only to persuade them to run away."

"Yes," Father said, "for a moment I had forgotten." His face looked haggard, but then became almost incredulous. "There is something going on, they are preparing a celebration. A wedding perhaps?"

"We shall know soon enough."

At the sight of the approaching carriage several Gypsy children broke away from the camp and ran towards us. The driver stopped at the end of the path, some distance away from the first wagon. I knew the man was reluctant to drive further. Fear of Gypsy magic and curses dies hard.

We took our valises down as the children reached us, shouting their welcome. Mara woke up and smiled as little girls welcomed her, calling her name.

Father paid the fare. The droshky drove off. Some boys grabbed our suitcases and dragged them in pairs, holding the handles from both sides, towards the camp. The others rushed ahead to inform my father's parents. We carried our instruments. I saw my grandfather, Sandu, stepping down from his wagon, a bent figure with a huge mane of white hair falling over his shoulders. My father ran to embrace him. There was a general commotion in the camp and several men and women, young and old alike,

32

rushed to greet us. There was a lot of handshaking and backslapping. "You came for the celebrations, didn't you?"

"What celebrations?" Father asked.

"The birthday. The fiftieth birthday of our leader, the Shero Rom. Isn't that why you have come?"

Father shook his head, bewildered, but said nothing. Accompanied by a throng of people and raucous children, and led by my grandfather, we made our way into the camp.

The large wagons, which had been bought from travelling circuses long ago and permanently placed here, their wheels partly buried in the ground, were spread in a circle, and in its middle there was one tent for the meetings of the Council of Elders, another for a workshop, and a huge one for sheltering the horses for the winter. But real winter had not yet come and several horses were outside tethered to their wagons, eating their fodder from wooden troughs. Mongrel dogs, which ran wild around the camp, formed a pack at the sight of our procession, and started barking and wagging their tails as if they too wanted to welcome the guests.

My grandfather mounted the three steps of his wagon and put his head into the door. "Rosa!" he shouted. "Dymitr is here. And Wala and the children!"

My grandmother stepped down from the wagon with outstretched arms. She kissed her son and daughter-in-law, then clasped her hands excitedly at the sight of my sister and me. "They have grown up, the children! You look like a man, Roman!" She hugged us both, a robust old woman with an enormous behind and ample bust, and a wind-furrowed, weather-beaten face. Her grey hair was tied back into a severe knot and covered with a red kerchief. "Come inside," she beckoned.

"I must go and greet my parents first," Mother said. "I'll be back soon." She left, a few children rushing ahead of her to be the first to inform her family.

There was little space inside my grandparents' wagon; still it was large enough to accommodate us all. The children carried the valises inside, then left, shooed off by my grandmother. We all sat down on stools. Over the two windows hung lace curtains. In the rear of the wagon stood a table with stacked china, an iron kettle and a few mugs, and above it on the wall hung a silver-framed picture of the Black Madonna of Częstochowa, adorned with artificial roses. The entire kumpania was Catholic. Pictures of various saints, interspersed with family photographs, decorated the inside of the wagon.

Father pulled out a silver case and offered cigarettes. Grandfather took one and let his son light it for him. Grandmother waved the case away and picked up her long clay pipe and filled it with crushed dried oak leaves. "You want some tea?" she asked. "There is going to be plenty of food and drink in an hour or so. A big celebration. The Shero Rom is only fifty years old once."

My father drew in a shuddering sigh. "We didn't come for the celebration unfortunately," he said, shifting uncomfortably on his seat as if debating with himself whether to delay what he had to say or to bring it up immediately. Then he turned to his father. "We have left Warsaw for good," he said. "They are catching Gypsies and putting them in the ghetto, then shipping them off to concentration camps. Just like the Jews. I came here to try and persuade all of you to run away."

My grandfather narrowed his eyes and shook his head. "Nothing is happening to the Gypsies here," he said. "Our girls go to town and to the Fortress every day, to dance for the Germans and tell them their fortunes. Our young men work in a concrete factory. We, the older ones, mend utensils or make new ones, as usual, and sell them to the Germans and the Poles. Nothing has happened to our neighbours, the Kelderari, the Coppersmith Gypsies from Terespol, either."

"Listen, please!" my father said. "Listen to me!" Then

he told my grandfather all he had heard from Danko, but the old man still could not comprehend.

"Maybe Danko, maybe the others who were in prison or in the ghetto, did something wrong. We Gypsies always manage to do something wrong – maybe they stole things or hit a German soldier. Listen, would German officers be coming here tonight for the festivities if there were any danger to us? Yes, we have invited them and they are coming – the colonel himself from the Fortress and others. You'll see."

Grandfather glanced at his wife. My grandmother had listened, but not uttered a word. Now it was her turn to speak. She was Pchuri Daj – the Clever Old Mother. She gave advice to the women, administered herbal medicine to the sick and taught the young girls how to tell fortunes to the gadje.

"Dymitr, you must see the Shero Rom," she said, "and tell him what you told us."

Father nodded reluctantly. "All right. Tomorrow. I'll talk to the Shero Rom tomorrow, first thing in the morning. No time must be lost."

A huge fire had been built in the centre of the camp and several rows of benches set around it. In the very front were four armchairs, three for the German officers and one for Mikita Kowal, the leader and chief judge of the kumpania. Also in the front were chairs for the Kelderari guests. Around the fire a wooden platform had been placed for the performers.

A little further away, by the river bank, stood tables laden with food and drink. Another fire was burning there in a big hole in the ground and inside it, among hot flat stones, lay a clay cube containing a hedgehog that was being slowly baked for the feast.

At eight in the evening a firework was shot high into the sky, breaking out into a beautiful star. This was the signal for the festivities to begin. From all the wagons Gypsies began streaming towards the benches, all dressed in their

35

best, the women in long, bright, multi-coloured robes with sequin necklaces, and the men in chequered cotton shirts, their collars over the lapels of their dark jackets, many of them wearing top boots. Some of the older people carried wrapped packages with them.

All of us, except for my father, took over the bench immediately behind the armchairs. We looked towards a large wagon, painted red and blue, with sculptured wooden dragons and griffins over its entrance, for we knew my father was in there, paying his respects to the Shero Rom. Finally he came out and joined us. "I said nothing, but I told him I must see him tomorrow morning to talk about an important matter." Earlier we had gone to greet my grandparents on my mother's side and now we waved to them as Antoni and Nina Puma took their seats on a nearby bench, the stocky little man and his equally small plump wife, her body marked by numerous childbearings, river laundering and cooking for her large family. "Tomorrow I'll also go and see Danko's parents," my father said. "But tonight let us forget our troubles." His face looked tense and I knew he could not dismiss the heavy burden from his mind.

The big throng now began to shout their welcome as two little houses on wheels appeared on the path leading to the camp. They were painted blue and green with carved and gilded fronts, their windows covered by lace curtains, the wheels hooped with iron and copper ornaments. The wagons stopped and from them descended a dozen Kelderari, the men dressed in baggy trousers and jackets adorned with silver buttons, the women in long tribal skirts composed of two overlapping gaily coloured pieces of cloth, and tight waistcoats with spangles of gold coins woven into long braids. The Kelderari had come to Poland from Transylvania a bare one hundred years ago. They tried to assert their superiority over the Lowland Gypsies – the Polska Roma – who had lived here for seven centuries, and to make them follow their customs and even change their religion from Catholic to Eastern Orthodox. But this particular group

36

was different. They were good neighbours and friends. Their chieftain, a tall bony-faced man wearing an overcoat and a felt borsalino, was carrying a huge ribbon-wrapped package, a gift for the Shero Rom. They were immediately ushered to their chairs. "Guests home, God home," their hosts welcomed them with the traditional greeting.

Now the entire crowd broke into applause, accompanied by shrill admiring whistles, as Mikita Kowal, the Shero Rom, finally made his appearance, emerging from his wagon with his son, Koro, walking respectfully one step behind him. Mikita was a widower and Koro his only son. Immediately two pretty long-limbed girls dashed to his armchair, flanking it, ready to respond to any request their Shero Rom might make. Mikita was a huge man, broad and heavy-set, with shoulder-length hair, a trim moustache and deeply set black eyes. He not only wore a tall sheepskin hat and a neat three-piece suit with a jacket that was somewhat too short, but also a bright red tie, and in his hand he held a long leather-plaited whip. Koro, who strongly resembled his father, was a youth of my age, curly-haired and husky, with the strong, muscled body of a young animal. He sat on a chair next to his father, acting very much like the crown prince. He glanced behind him once to size up the crowd, and his eyes fell on me. I waved to him. With a dignified nod of his head, Koro acknowledged my presence. I knew he did not like me and looked down on me, always treating me as though I were a traitor to my tribe.

Another firework was shot into the air, just as a Volkswagen car appeared on the path to the encampment. The Shero Rom rose from his chair and rushed forward. Three German officers alighted and, when they saluted, Mikita raised his hand to his hat, returning the salute. "Thank you, Colonel Krüger, for coming," he said in German, bowing a few times as he led his guests to their chairs. The blond and blue-eyed colonel, in his early fifties, a monocle in his left eye, took the seat next to Mikita. His two aides sat in the two other armchairs.

37

"This is my son, Koro." Mikita proudly introduced the boy. Krüger glanced at the young Gypsy and nodded approvingly. Mikita rubbed his hands with satisfaction, for the arrival of the German officers enhanced his status. Then he shouted, "Let us begin!"

Suddenly music was heard. All heads turned as, from the darkness of the woods, a band emerged, playing 'Sto lat!', strolling towards the camp-fire. The Gypsy audience broke into the Polish birthday song, clapping their hands in rhythm as they wished their chief a hundred-years-long life. The Shero Rom rose from his chair and waved both his hat and his whip to express his thanks. The band – several violinists, a mandolinist and a flautist – reached the middle of the circle, paused for a moment until the applause died down, and then began playing a lilting melody, 'The Old Gypsy'.

Mikita smiled benevolently, because for a Gypsy to be told he was old was no offence; it also meant to be wise and respected. "You like django, Colonel Krüger?" he asked. "The Gypsy music."

The colonel nodded slightly, his face reserved and impassive. I was sitting directly behind Mikita and Krüger and could hear what they said.

"I hope you also like our food." Mikita pointed to the tables. "We'll eat in a while, but before the meal there will be a little ceremony."

It was the Kelderari chief who stepped out first, carrying a package. He bowed to Colonel Krüger, saying, "Guten Abend," and the colonel, who obviously knew him, answered, "Guten Abend, Dombrowski." Then the man approached the Shero Rom and handed him the gift. "May you and your horses live long," he said in the Romany language.

"Thank you, my friend," Mikita answered.

From all the benches around the fire circle now came the older men, each representing his own clan and carrying their presents. A huge pile soon rose on the ground in front

38

of their chief. Grandfather brought the Shero Rom three tea mugs and Father came over too, because he was a guest, offering Mikita two of his ties. When no one any longer stepped forward, the Shero Rom ordered the two girls to bring food for the German officers and for himself, while all the others waited out of respect.

The girls ran to the tables, the two young officers eyeing their supple, long-waisted, nimble figures. "We have many Gypsies in Germany." Krüger turned to Mikita. "They call themselves Sinti. Quite a number of them are serving on the Russian front."

I saw Mikita Kowal beam with pride, but I recalled what Danko had told us about the five thousand Sinti who were brought to the Łódź ghetto, dying of typhus by the hundred, and the survivors being sent on to the Chelmno concentration camp. I looked questioningly at my father who had also been listening to the conversation in front of us. "Perhaps those on the front are Diddakoi – half-Gypsies," he whispered to me. "Or married to German women. Who knows?"

The girls returned, carrying four laden trays, and offered them to the Germans and Mikita. There was a bowl of soup on each tray, slices of black bread and dark Gypsy ham, pickles and a glass, half-filled with a burgundy-coloured drink. "This is wiśniak," the Shero Rom said, raising his glass. "We brew it ourselves from wild cherries. Prosit!"

"Prosit!" the Germans answered. "Very good," Colonel Krüger complimented Mikita after carefully tasting the alcohol. Then he drank it all in a few gulps as if it were schnaps. "Good and strong!" Immediately Mikita sent a girl to refill the colonel's glass, then he clapped his hands, a signal for the whole kumpania to start towards the tables. They led their Kelderari guests in front and soon a huge, colourful crowd gathered on the river bank, eating, drinking and laughing.

The officers now picked up their spoons and began to eat

their soup. "Very good," Krüger said again. "A vegetable soup, eh?"

The Shero Rom didn't have a spoon; he didn't need one. He raised his bowl to his mouth, slurping the liquid with noisy approval. "Nettle soup. Delicious, right?" he said.

The colonel picked up his refilled glass, which the Gypsy girl had just brought, and took a good swallow.

A man, dressed brightly in a waistcoat with golden buttons and wearing several bead necklaces, pushed a wheelbarrow decorated with gold and silver papier-mâché in the direction of the tables. In it lay the clay cube and a stack of large leaves. He halted in front of the Shero Rom and his German guests. "What's that?" Krüger asked, adjusting his monocle for a better look, while the Gypsy began breaking the clay by hammering a screwdriver into it in several places. He put on thick gloves and pulled the clay pieces apart. The prickles and skin of the hedgehog had become attached to the clay and the white meat of the animal was now exposed, ready to be served. The man cut a portion, placed it on a leaf and passed it on to Mikita, who in turn offered it to the colonel. "Niglo," he said. "Our supreme delicacy. It is at its best now because it picks up fat for the winter sleep." He smacked his lips with gusto.

The German shuddered and returned his offering to Mikita. "No, thank you."

"Please try some. Believe me – it's better than chicken, or partridge, or pheasant."

"I believe you, but our stomachs are not accustomed to it." He looked at his military aides and the officers exchanged a wry smile. Mikita started to eat, turning his deep eyeballs heavenwards to show how delectable the hedgehog meat was, but he could not convince the Germans. Mikita lowered his head, disappointed, then told the cook to serve the meat to the Kelderari men. There was not enough of it for everybody.

The band kept playing, switching from tune to tune,

40

while more fireworks were let off. The crowd returned to their benches around the camp-fire, waiting for the performance to begin.

From one of the tents appeared a line of girls in ankle-length robes. When they reached the platform, they spread out into three rows and began to dance with little steps, moving slightly forward and sideways, their bodies immobile, only their hands moving, joining, parting and thrusting forward. To the accompaniment of the music – the strumming of the mandolin, the melodic harmony of the flute and the foot-stomping rhythm of the fiddle – the girls danced faster and faster, their arms moving more and more swiftly, until they reached the climax of their dance, with their hands abruptly dropping, their fingers fluttering like the wings of dying birds.

There was loud applause; the dancers dispersed to take their places with their families, while a boy brought out the Gypsy cymbals, and a very old man, his face weathered by sun, wind and time, sat on a stool and struck an iron rod against the movable rings strung on the steel wires of his triangular instrument. The cymbals were followed by a wrestling match as two young men, stripped to their shorts, introduced themselves to the guests by bowing and announcing their names as Rudolf Puma and Jan Michalak. I smiled at my mother who was leaning forward excitedly. Rudolf was her brother.

"Where is the judge?" one of the officers asked.

"Here." Mikita, the chief judge of the kumpania, pointed at himself.

The two men, their heads bent, their arms at the ready, began walking slowly around each other, like hunters stalking their prey. Finally, Rudolf wound his arms around Jan and pressed his chin against him in the opposite direction to force him to his knees. Jan resisted fiercely. Their clinch lasted a few minutes. The wrestlers now looked like two bulls engaged in mortal combat, their bodies soaked in sweat and glistening in the light of the camp-fire. The

41

audience broke into two opposing camps, shouting encouragement to whichever of the two wrestlers they supported.

Suddenly Jan threw his leg forward and succeeded in tripping his opponent to the ground. Immediately he threw himself on Rudolf, but Wala's brother managed to entwine his legs and hands over those of his adversary and the two men began rolling over the platform, sometimes Rudolf, sometimes Jan on top. After a while they broke apart and both jumped to their feet simultaneously.

Once more they circled each other, then suddenly Rudolf bent down, grabbed both of Jan's legs, and threw him on the ground, then fell astraddle over him, his large hands pressing down on Jan's shoulders. The audience rose to their feet. Wala, all red-faced, shouted, "Hold him down, hold him!" Jan desperately managed to move first the left shoulder, then the right away from the floor, but finally Rudolf succeeded in pressing both shoulders down not only with his arms, but with his knees as well. "One, two, three!" Mikita Kowal said, counting from the time both of Jan's shoulders touched the ground. Then the Shero Rom got up and pronounced Rudolf Puma the winner. The audience broke into applause. The wrestlers got up, Rudolf victoriously raised his hands, and then both men left the platform, returning to their wagons to dress.

The German officers' glasses were refilled with wiśniak as a girl dressed in a flowing red skirt and a tight black bolero came out for a solo. At first she moved slowly around the fire to the rhythm of her castanets, as if presenting herself to the audience. I leaned forward. The girl had a delicate copper-coloured face, perfectly sculptured lips, a small straight nose and black, almond-shaped eyes. I felt my heart miss a beat; never before had I seen such beauty, not amongst the Gypsies, not even amongst the gadje.

The girl now raised her hands, clicking her castanets above her head, swaying her body and stamping her feet as she moved faster and faster in what was an imitation of the flamenco of the Gitanos, the Spanish Gypsies. Eagerly I followed the slim, adolescent dancing body, with its extremely long waist, the girl's slender hips outlined under her billowing cotton skirt. "Who is she?" I asked, my voice uncertain. My parents did not know, but my grandmother said, "Zoya, Zoya Natkin."

"I didn't see her last year."

"Last year," Grandmother's pale lips curved into a smile, "she was thirteen. She is a woman now."

The sound of castanets filled the air as the girl beat the rhythm with her heels, time and again whirling rapidly around, bringing the dance to a crescendo. The music halted abruptly and Zoya sank to one knee, bowing her head for the expected applause. People shouted, "Bravo! Bravo!", clapping their hands wildly, and I noticed that Koro was shouting louder and clapping more excitedly than anyone else in the crowd.

The girl left with quick shuffling steps, but the image of her outstretched savage body and her oriental beauty stayed with me, while a group of dancing men and women took her place on the platform.

They were all dressed in blue costumes with little bells sewn on to them; they wore spurs on their feet and were armed with sticks. "The final number," Mikita told Colonel Krüger. "The dance of the Kalus, the Romanian Gypsies." The dance did not last long and when the dancers scattered from the platform, Mikita, his face red from excitement and alcohol, raised his glass of wiśniak to the colonel. "Did you enjoy it?" he asked.

"Yes," the German said. "One day you must send your dancers and wrestlers to the Fortress to perform for our garrison."

"Gladly," Mikita answered. "Gladly!"

"And now," Colonel Krüger said, "I would like to say a few words to your people. Could you please translate to them what I have to say."

"Certainly." Mikita got up and followed the colonel to

43

the middle of the circle, his face full of expectation of the forthcoming compliments and expressions of thanks.

"Damen und Herren," Krüger started. He then continued in German, saying that he too had not come empty-handed. He had also brought a gift to the Shero Rom, to all of them.

After every few sentences he stopped for Mikita's translation. "This winter is going to be very hard," the German officer said, "and I would like to pass on to you the kind offer of the Ostland, the East-Land authorities, to settle all the Gypsies in lovely warm houses. You won't have to freeze in your wooden wagons any longer. There are apartments, each of a few rooms, with hot and cold running water and glazed tile stoves and a bathroom and a water closet *inside* the house – waiting for you."

"Where is that?" the Shero Rom asked, interrupting his translation.

"In the houses of Brest Litovsk where the Jews used to live."

I saw my father lifting himself slightly from his seat. "Where are those Jews now?" he asked loudly.

"Resettled," Krüger answered, without batting an eyelid. My father opened his mouth to speak again, then, with a sigh, closed it. "The Kelderari will also live there," Krüger went on. "Right, Dombrowski?"

The chieftain of the Coppersmiths rose. "Right, Colonel. We will be moving there this week – and thank you."

"Let me make one thing quite clear," Colonel Krüger said. "The Jews are an inferior race, they have made trouble for Christians all through the centuries. But you *are* Christians, you are Aryans, like us. We shall not treat you in any way different from the Poles." He turned to Mikita. "Do you accept our offer?"

The Shero Rom scrutinised the faces of his people. "Tomorrow," he said finally, "I will give you our answer. I shall call a meeting of the Council of Elders and what they decide will also be my decision."

44

"Fine," Krüger said. "I'll be expecting you tomorrow to give me your answer. And I hope it will be the same one as Dombrowski's. For your own sake. I repeat, it's going to be a very hard, frosty winter."

"Winters are bad," the Shero Rom answered. "We have a saying that it's better to live through one summer than seven winters. I hope to bring you a yes answer tomorrow."

"Good. And now I must leave." The colonel raised his hand in a military salute and again Mikita answered by touching his sheepskin hat. The two junior officers rose, too.

Mikita accompanied his German guests to their car. "Thank you, Colonel, for coming," he said. "And for your kind offer." He waited, waving his whip until the Volkswagen disappeared from view.

Mara meanwhile had fallen asleep in her mother's arms and now, with the Germans gone, Mother said, "I'm exhausted, too. I'm taking the girl and myself to bed."

"We split like in the past, right?" Father asked. "You and Mara with your parents, Roman and I with mine?"

"Yes," Mother said, "it's all arranged. Good night."

Father helped her to lift the girl, but Mara woke up, her arms clutching her mother's neck as she preferred to be carried.

The musicians now left the platform for all those who wanted to dance, finding a spot for themselves. From behind the crowd came sudden Gypsy laughter. I stood up and saw that a wheel of each of the two Kelderari wagons had been taken off and hidden, preventing the Coppersmiths from leaving, just as they were ready to go. It was a sign that my people had enjoyed the company of their guests so much that they wanted them to stay. "All right," I heard Dombrowski say. "But just an hour, no more. Make sure the wheels are back on by then." The Kelderari returned to their chairs and some, younger ones, went to the floor to dance as wildly as their hosts.

45

My grandfather rose from his place. "Let the youngsters dance till dawn," he said. "There was a time when I would stay and outdance them all, but that time has passed. Rosa and I are going to turn in."

"I want to be fresh for tomorrow's talk with the Shero Rom," Father said. "He, too, is retiring." I looked and saw the two girls collecting the presents and carrying them after Mikita walking towards his tent. "Come, Roman," Father said. "Tomorrow is another day – and a very important one."

I wanted to stay, to catch another glimpse of the girl who danced like the Gitanos of Spain, but she was nowhere to be seen. I felt very tired what with only a few hours of sleep the previous night, the long journey, the food, the excitement, and all my mixed emotions. Obediently I followed my father and grandparents to their wagon.

The kerosene lamp was lit inside and bedding had been made up for us all. When we lay down, Grandfather blew out the light. Sleepy though I had been a moment ago, I kept tossing and turning, listening to the wind which suddenly got up, battering the canvas of the nearby tents. Warsaw, the school, the night club, our apartment in the Praga suburb – all suddenly seemed long ago and far away. The Gypsies and their dancers and their Shero Rom were here and now. And what stood out above all was the vision of the girl who had danced the dance of the Gitanos, completely erasing from my mind the flaxen-haired braids and the blue eyes of the Polish waitress at Fukier's Wine Cellar.

The snoring and wheezing of my grandparents told me that they were asleep, but then the dim, hazy light in the wagon was blocked out by the tall figure of my father going outside. I followed him. "You can't sleep?" I asked.

He leaned against the wagon and lit a cigarette, perhaps one of the last packs saved from Warsaw. "I'm thinking of the ghetto," he said. "I am sure they want to put us all there, behind barbed wire, so that they can easily gather us up in trucks and take us to a concentration camp. I must not let it happen. We must leave at once, tomorrow."

"Yes, Father."

"You'll come with me to the Shero Rom, to confirm, if necessary, everything I tell him. But don't talk unless I ask you."

"I'll do as you say, Father."

We both fell silent. The wind blew through the branches of the trees as we, lost in our private thoughts, watched the splashes of colour dancing before our eyes near the camp-fire and listened to the laughter and merry voices, and to the thud of stamping boots and hip-slapping which accompanied the lilting cry of the Gypsy violins.

3

My father pointed at a small fire burning outside the wagon, a black iron kettle hanging over it. "He is up," he said to me, then shouted, "Shero Rom, it's Dymitr! Can we come in?"

"Come in!" answered the booming voice from inside the wagon.

Mikita was already dressed, sitting at a table with a cup of hot tea. He rose from his chair and shook hands with my father and me, then took two more cups and saucers out of a cupboard. "I'll get you some tea. Sit down." In a moment he was back with the kettle and poured the boiling liquid for us, then opened a silver box, offering us lumps of sugar.

I had never seen inside the Shero Rom's wagon. The floor was covered with thick colourful carpets. Two iron beds with chequered bedspreads stood on each side of a large wooden wardrobe. As in the wagons of other Gypsies, holy and family pictures hung together on the walls, most of them silver- and tin-framed.

Mikita poured tea into his saucer. My father did the same and his look urged me to follow his example. "You had a splendid birthday," Father said. "Only people who love their Shero Rom could have arranged it so beautifully."

"Thank you, Dymitr. And it was nice of you to remember it. Usually, you come home for Christmas." Mikita raised the saucer and noisily sipped some tea. "You said you had an important matter to discuss with me."

"Very important. The night before yesterday, when we

48

returned home from our night club, we found Danko Mular waiting for us. He was covered with blood and his clothes were torn. He had just escaped from a prison in the Warsaw ghetto."

Mikita's hand with the saucer stopped in mid-air. "You mean they have also taken away the Warsaw Jews and given Gypsies their houses?"

"They took many Jews away to concentration camps, Treblinka mostly, but not all of them – not yet. The Gypsies live there *alongside* the Jews. Danko had previously been in the Łódź ghetto where there were tens of thousands of Jews, but also about 5,000 Sinti. I heard Colonel Krüger say that the Sinti are fighting in the German Wehrmacht. Maybe a few are, but there are others in the Łódź ghetto. They were decimated by typhus, and those who managed to live through the epidemic were sent to Chelmno, another concentration camp. Danko escaped to Warsaw, but then he was caught there."

"There are 30,000 Sinti," Mikita answered. "What about the other 25,000? I'm sure they live in Germany in peace. Look, Dymitr, we Gypsies like our own way of life and often pay no attention to what the gadje orders us to do. But we must be reasonable and obey when there is no way to disobey. That's how we've survived all the persecutions of the past thousand years. Drink, your tea will get cold."

My father put the lump of sugar into his mouth and, holding it there, drank the liquid from the saucer, making as much noise as possible to show his host that he was enjoying it. Between sips he continued telling Mikita everything that Danko had told him.

Mikita filled his pipe with real tobacco and lit it. "Danko is your cousin, but I've known him since he was born. He is a real spinner of tales, always was. Maybe he told you all that to cover up his own misbehaviour? Who knows? Maybe he got into a fight with a German?"

"He did. That's why they put him in prison."

49

"You see. And maybe the same thing happened before in Łódź. Anyway, where is he now? Why didn't he come and tell us this himself?"

"He fled to the forest near Warsaw, to form a Gypsy partisan band to fight the Germans."

Mikita smiled. "This also I don't believe. Another tale. We Gypsies are brave and wild, but not so crazy as to fight Germans with their guns and tanks." Father took the last sip of tea, then put his empty cup on its side in the saucer, indicating he wanted no more. "Look, Dymitr," Mikita went on, "did you see the German officers here yesterday, drinking with us, eating with us, enjoying our music and dances? And what did the commander of the garrison himself, a personal friend of mine, tell us? That we mustn't compare ourselves with the Jews. We are Christians, we are Aryans, like the Germans themselves. Isn't that what he said? And then being so kind as to offer us warm houses for the winter?"

Father shut his eyes and shook his head, annoyed. "Oh, God, and you believe *him*? Not me, not Danko, but this Colonel Krüger? Do you know what will happen to you if you accept his offer? There is barbed wire all around the ghetto, isn't there? And once you are inside, you may not be able to get out. The next thing you know, a column of trucks will arrive to pick you all up and transport you to Chelmno or Treblinka."

"Tumri," Mikita said. "It's all nonsense. Fear has big eyes. They took the Jews from the ghetto here, all of them, but what happened to us? Nothing. Our young men work in a German concrete factory and even get paid a bit, our women move around freely, telling fortunes. We are even invited to the Fortress to perform for their garrison. Whatever happened to some Gypsy troublemakers won't happen to us. We here enjoy the best of relations with the Germans. You go back to Warsaw, to your night club, and don't worry about us. We are gawitka and weszytka Roma – village and forest Gypsies. We'll winter here and in the

50

spring resume our travelling from village to village and forest to forest, as usual, and when you visit us next year for Christmas, you'll see us all back here, safe and sound."

My father looked at me as if wishing to summon my help, but then said, "Mikita, you must pack and start travelling now. We must get to Hungary. There are no Germans there and no danger to us."

"Are you crazy, Dymitr? You want us to travel in the winter? We'll freeze to death on the way. And even if some of us manage to get to Hungary, what shall we do there? You are a musician, you may find a job, but what shall the rest of us do in Hungary? We don't even speak their language."

My father looked at me again, helplessly. "Why don't you at least put the matter to the Council of Elders? At the same time that you present them with the German offer of the ghetto houses?"

For a while Mikita remained pensive. He drew on his pipe, then said, "All right, Dymitr Mirga. I will do that. Right after our noontime meal. You come and state your case, I will state mine. I will listen to their advice and then will announce my decision."

The sun came out and the patches of snow on the ground melted. Men worked in front of their wagons, repairing pots and cauldrons or fashioning chains, axes and sickles for sale to Polish, Byelorussian and Ukrainian peasants. The air was filled with sparks that flew high. Even if my father was unable to convince the Shero Rom, he would certainly manage to persuade the wise Elders, I thought.

I was taking a stroll through the camp, hoping to catch a glimpse of the girl who had danced so excitingly the previous night. I stopped to greet Gregory Mular hammering a shoe on to his horse. Danko's father was a big, muscular man, only his white hair and beard betraying his old age. "My father is coming to see you soon," I said.

51

"Good." The old man finished his work and slapped his horse on the rump, sending it towards the river to drink. As my eyes followed the animal, I noticed a string of girls on the river bank, doing their laundry.

"Good morning, Roman," I heard and saw Zela, Danko's mother, who was wearing big sequin earrings, come out of her wagon, sweeping the dirt and dust out with her broom. "Nice sunny morning."

"It's going to be a good day," I answered absent-mindedly. My eyes had focused on the last girl on the right, for I recognised her long, slim back and dark shoulder-length hair. "Nice to see you both," I said. I started towards the river, but because I was anxious my movements were swift and sudden, and the dogs, startled, ran after me, barking. The girls looked up from the clothes they were washing to see what all the commotion was about. When they saw me they started to giggle, but as I approached them, they quickly composed their faces and began rubbing the clothes harder on the scrubbing boards. Near each of them lay two piles of clothing. Gypsies never mix male and female clothes when washing them; and they never use soap, so their work is harder.

I pretended that I had just come to look at the river flowing by. I stopped close to Zoya, picked up a few pebbles and casually tried to make rings on the surface of the water. I sneaked a glance at the squatting girl and met her slightly raised face with a curious glance in her black eyes and a tiny smile on her opened lips, showing a set of perfect small white teeth. She looked down quickly before I at last summoned my courage to say, "Good morning, Zoya. You danced beautifully last night. I didn't know you were a Gitana."

The girl laughed in response. "Neither did I," she said. "You are Roman Mirga from Warsaw, yes?"

"Yes," I said, speaking in a low voice so that the others would not hear. "You have grown up very quickly since the last time I saw you." My eyes fell on her small but firm bosom, like two snowballs, stretching her white blouse. I saw Zoya blush and quickly flipped a pebble held in my hand, making it skim the water. "Can you make rings?"

"I don't know, I never tried."

Some of the girls started to pick up their finished laundry and leave. "Well, try now."

Zoya wrung the water from a dress she had just washed, then put it on top of the pile of female clothes. She took a pebble from my hand and, giggling, threw it. The little stone sank immediately. "No, I'm no good at that. You have finished school?"

"No. One more year to go. I doubt if I'll finish, though."

"Why? It's good for a man to finish school."

"We are not going back to Warsaw."

"Why?" She threw me a strange sidelong glance. "Have you come home for good?"

"Yes, I think so."

Zoya put a blouse on the scrubbing board and worked on it for a while. It was the last piece of clothing she had to wash. I searched for words to say something, but they eluded me so I just stood there tongue-tied until I saw her wring the water from the blouse. "Your family's laundry?"

"Yes, mine, my parents' and my brother's." She pushed one set of clothes under her arm and was about to do the same with the other.

"Let me help you," I said.

I saw the girl's face suddenly become tense, the skin on her forehead tightening as she looked into the distance. "No need," she said, "I can manage."

I glanced over my shoulder and saw Koro Kowal some fifty metres away, in front of his wagon, staring at us.

"Ira!" I heard Zoya call to a girl carrying her laundry back home. "Wait for me!" With her own load under her arms, she quickly joined her friend, leaving me behind without uttering another word.

53

I continued watching the river for a while, then turned and walked slowly back towards my grandparents' wagon.

We men had our meal at a table set outside the wagon, one dish as usual and as fat as possible as usual. My grandmother had prepared bigos – sauerkraut with slices of lard and sausages – especially for her son and me, because we both loved it. My father pulled out his watch. "Time," he said. "Let's go."

My grandfather and I rose. The women now sat down, ready to eat. "Be firm," Mother said to my father. "Well, I don't have to tell you. I know you will."

On our way to the tent where the Council of Elders was meeting, my father turned to my grandfather. "I'm counting on your help."

"I shall not speak against you."

My father stopped, startled. I looked incredulously at my grandfather. "What do you mean, you won't speak against me? I expect you to speak for me," my father said.

"I told you yesterday, we are in no danger here," my grandfather answered. "Maybe in Warsaw and Łódź, in the big cities, but not here. So it's good that you left and came home."

"But Grandmother asked Father to see the Shero Rom," I interjected, my voice rising.

"Because he is the wisest of all, he is the head of the kumpania."

"This morning, this very morning," my father went on angrily, "when I came back from him, you said nothing. Mother said nothing."

"What was there to say? He said the same thing as I." My grandfather put his hand on Father's shoulder. "You are our son. That's why I promise not to say anything, to keep silent. You will see, the Elders will be of the same opinion."

"Gregory Mular said he would support me."

"All right – one man, father of Danko."

"You are father of Dymitr."

"But what does Dymitr know? Nothing. Only what Danko has told him. Believe me, son, I am a wise old man. The devil is not as black as he's painted."

We saw Koro coming towards us, and stopped talking, resuming our walk. Koro wore top boots, a knife sticking out of the right one, its blade glistening in the midday sun. He hesitated as if wanting to say something, but then continued, passing us without a word.

Shaking his head to himself in disbelief, my father entered the big tent before his father, forgetting about paying the customary respect to the Elders.

In the tent, two rows of chairs, four to a row, had been arranged. Mikita sat in his armchair, playing with his whip and facing five old men. "Sit there, Dymitr." He pointed to a small bench, just large enough for two. Grandfather joined the other Elders. "Filip and Tomasz are still not here," Mikita said. "I sent Tomasz to take a good look at the ghetto houses, but he should have been back by now. Will somebody fetch Filip Kuchar?"

"Filip is ill," Szura Greczko, the oldest man in the camp said. He was bald on the top of his head with loose bushy white hair on both sides and a soft, rosy, oval face. "He has a high fever."

Mikita rubbed his chin. "I don't want to start with just six of you and myself. We will wait for Tomasz."

"With Dymitr and his son we are nine in the tent," Gregory said.

"Yes, that's true. We are nine. Let's start then." I glanced furtively at my father. Nine was lucky, seven unlucky. Superstitions, always superstitions. "We are gathered here," Mikita went on, "to consider Colonel Krüger's offer of houses for the winter and also what Dymitr Mirga is going to tell us."

"On the matter of houses . . ." said a man called Zenon Cysin. He was the only one who wore a red kerchief tied to one side. "I want to speak on the matter of houses."

Mikita waved his hand. "No, let's wait for Tomasz. Meanwhile let Dymitr speak."

My father got up. He sized up the faces of all the Elders, then began. He spoke for a long time, missing no detail of what Danko had told him. "That's why I came here," he said. "To warn you about the terrible danger and suggest that we all leave at once." He outlined his plan of going wesz weszestyr, from forest to forest, until reaching Hungary, while this was still possible. "And so," he concluded, "if you decide to leave, there is no need to discuss Krüger's offer."

"Right," Gregory chimed in.

"The Elders do not decide," Mikita reminded him. "They advise, I decide. So now I want to tell you what I think about all this, and then you can speak your mind. I say, fear has big eyes. In that Łódź ghetto, where Danko saw five thousand Gypsies, I am sure there were no more than five hundred. They probably disobeyed orders, maybe refused to join labour brigades. The Germans do take young people to work in their factories, on the railways and roads. Like here, where we have most of our young men working in their concrete factory. But there are plenty amongst other tribes, amongst the Sinti, especially the Lalleri Sinti, the 'dumb Gypsies', who say that life is too short for a Gypsy to work."

"Danko would not say five thousand unless there were five thousand," Gregory interjected. "My son doesn't lie."

Mikita smiled tolerantly. "If he were my son, Gregory, I would have said the same. But I have known Danko as long as you. Since he was born. I do not mean he lies, he just exaggerates. He always liked telling tall stories – about Polish girls who fell in love with him, about noblemen who invited him to their mansions for dinner and wine."

"That's not the same. This is a serious matter, a matter of life and death."

"They grow soft," Szura Greczko said, "once they settle

56

in big towns. They easily get frightened and spread rumours."

"I never trusted town Poles and the same goes for town Gypsies," Zenon Cysin added.

"I am also from town," my father said angrily. "Just like Danko. Don't you trust me?"

"Of course we trust you," the Shero Rom said. "But all you know comes from Danko. I am not only the head of the kumpania, Dymitr, I am also the chief judge of it. I can't base my decision on hearsay. Here we obey the Germans. They wanted our young men to work for them, and so they work for them. That's why our situation is different and nothing will happen to us. To those who disobey, or those who are caught stealing and committing crimes, yes. But not to us. We are peaceful people and we obey the law. That's why Colonel Krüger is a personal friend of mine; he appreciates our help in their war effort."

"Yes," Szura Greczko said. "We don't make trouble, we don't get into trouble."

"We are Aryans, not Jews," the pot-bellied and be-whiskered Franko Zbar remarked.

"They invited us to come to the Fortress, to dance and wrestle for them," Zenon Cysin said.

"And they have offered us warm houses," the Shero Rom added quickly.

"That's different," Szura said. "I don't want houses for us. They have toilets inside them, not outside. Inside! They stink and probably bring many diseases."

"And they have bath tubs," another man, Zdenko Grabowski, said. "Who needs a bath if we have a river?"

"It is a different way of life. Fine for Dymitr and his family," Szura continued, "but in all my ninety years I haven't lived in a house and I won't start now."

"We are not discussing the houses now," Mikita interrupted. "I saw that some of you didn't look too happy last night when Colonel Krüger made the offer, and that is why I said what you will decide, I will decide. So in case

57

we don't accept it, I won't be blamed. I'll say it's your decision, the decision of the Elders. Anyway, we will discuss this when Tomasz comes back. Now I want to speak on the matter of Dymitr's proposal."

"I think as you do," Franko Zbar said. "Also – we have never travelled in the winter."

"That's what I said to Dymitr," Mikita quickly interposed. "We will freeze to death. And as I said, even if we get to Hungary, we don't know the language. His violin is his language, but only a few of us are musicians and dancers. And how will our women tell fortunes? In Polish?"

There was a rustle behind the men. They turned their heads at the sight of Tomasz Klimko, dressed smartly for town with a tie and a felt hat on his head. "I have been there, Shero Rom," he said.

"Wait a moment. We are talking now about . . ." Then he stopped. "Oh, all right, tell us what you saw."

Tomasz wiped his face. "The German soldiers watching over the area let me in. I walked around the ghetto, that's why it took me so long. All around it there is barbed wire. There is only one way of getting in or out – through a gate on Jagello Street. The soldiers let me see a few houses. There is no furniture in any of them. The Germans took it all."

"We don't need any furniture," Mikita observed.

"The houses smell terribly. Nobody cleaned them after they took the Jews away."

"We can clean them," Mikita said. "Look," he addressed all the Elders, "why did the Kelderari accept the offer? They are moving in any day now."

"Why don't we wait and see if they like it?" Tomasz suggested.

"And see what happens to the Kelderari," Gregory added wryly.

"All right," Mikita concluded. "I will tell Colonel Krüger that we have never lived in houses and want to wait and see if the Kelderari are happy in them. And I will tell

58

him that this was your decision." The Elders nodded their approval. "Now on the other matter, what do you advise? I want to hear each one of you."

They spoke in turn. Zenon Cysin, Szura Greczko and Franko Zbar all said they should remain in their winter encampment and not move. Zdenko Grabowski suggested that if things got worse, they could start travelling towards Hungary in the spring, since they would have to travel anyway.

"If you live that long," my father remarked with harsh sarcasm.

Gregory, father of Danko, rose to his feet. He believed in his son's and Dymitr's warning, he said. Would Dymitr have come all the way from Warsaw, would he have left his home and place of work unless the danger was really great? The Germans are clever – they don't start in all places at once. First Łódź, then Warsaw, then other towns and villages. Do the Elders, does the Shero Rom, believe that the Germans would limit their action to town Gypsies and leave nomadic tribes alone? He sat back, wiping away a few drops of sweat that had appeared on his forehead.

"Tomasz," Mikita said. "You haven't spoken yet."

"I wasn't here when you discussed the matter," Tomasz answered. "But I support the Shero Rom whatever he decides. Always."

"Sandu," Mikita said. "I haven't heard from you. You have said nothing so far."

"And I will say nothing now," my grandfather answered. "It's my son's proposal we are discussing and I don't think it is proper for his father to speak."

Mikita rose from his place. "You have all spoken," he said. "Or had a chance to speak. Now it's up to me to decide. I am responsible for you all, for all my people. And my decision is that we stay."

"You are wrong, Shero Rom!" I found myself shouting as I saw my father's face turn grim, his eyelids closing in despair.

59

Mikita glanced at me. "You didn't speak all this time, boy," he said, "and you will not speak now. I repeat, it's my decision to stay, not to move. You, Dymitr, can go back to Warsaw with your family."

"I cannot go back and I will not go back," my father said brusquely.

"That's for you to decide. I now declare the meeting of the Council of Elders closed."

The old men began to leave. My father looked around as if in a bad dream, then shook his head as if he could hardly believe that his plan to talk his people into running away, to save his relatives and friends, had been given this mortal blow. He got heavily to his feet. On our way out, my grandfather joined us. "What you sow today," Father said in anguish, "you shall reap tomorrow. You may pay heavily for the Shero Rom's decision."

Outside the tent, Gregory Mular approached us. "I didn't know you would keep silent," he said, pointing an accusing finger at my grandfather.

"Even if I'd spoken, would that have helped? All the other Elders but you were against the plan and so was the Shero Rom. Are you going to leave, Gregory?"

"No," Gregory said unhappily. "I would not go without the others. I've never travelled without my people."

"And you, Father?" my father asked as we started to walk back towards our wagon. "Will you come along, if I decide that we, Wala, the children and I, should leave?"

"We are too old to travel in the winter, son. Too old. And I hope that you won't go either. You are safe here; maybe not in Warsaw, but here you are safe." My father tightened his lips, and said nothing more.

We halted outside Gregory's wagon. Feebly he raised his hand, bidding goodbye to us. I looked searchingly into my father's face as we walked on among the howling dogs and neighing horses and thick-legged children playing outside their wagons.

Just as we were close to reaching our home, I saw Koro

Kowal coming out of the wagon where Zoya Natkin lived with her family. The son of the Shero Rom was walking straight towards us as if he had been waiting for our return. "The meeting finished?" he asked.

"Yes," my father answered. "Your father decided to stay."

"Good," Koro said. He turned abruptly to me. "I want to talk to you, Roman Mirga." His voice was strong and firm, brooking no opposition. "Alone."

My father turned questioningly to me. "All right," I said. "Alone." Father waved his hand and walked ahead, my grandfather, with a glance over his shoulder, following him.

Koro and I remained behind. "You'd better . . ." Koro snapped, fiercely thrusting his chin out, his fingers touching the handle of the knife sticking out of his top boot. "You'd better stay away from my girl."

"I don't know what you mean," I answered.

"I saw you talking to her this morning," Koro went on. "She has been promised to me, you understand? By her parents. We are getting married in the spring when she is fifteen."

"I didn't know," I muttered.

"Well, you do now. So keep away, I said." For a moment Koro looked straight into my eyes as if trying to impress his warning upon me, then he left, going back to Zoya Natkin's wagon.

I remained glued to the spot, my throat tightening. I felt an impotent rage. A gawitka and weszytka Roma, I thought with scorn. But how could I take all this? How could I accept the prejudices and superstitions and parental agreements and a soapless, caravan existence after living most of my life like the rest of the world? All of the world except for the Gypsies – and the Bedouins!

But my anger at Koro quickly dissipated as I walked home. There were more important things on my mind. Behind my grandparents' wagon my father was squatting

61

over a stack of branches and striking a flint to start a fire. The wood caught quickly. "What did Koro want?" he asked.

"Oh, nothing." I managed a wry smile. "Just to welcome me to the camp. What are you doing here?"

"Warming up the ground," my father answered. "Once it is done, we shall build a wooden hut over it. For us, for the winter."

"We are not going then?"

"No, son. I can't run away. I can't leave my parents. I'll stay and do all in my power to persuade them to go. Perhaps this stubborn old father of mine will realise that I am right. Or perhaps we shall indeed manage to stay safe until the winter is over."

4

Several weeks had passed since our arrival in the camp. Nothing had happened to us and Mikita Kowal missed no opportunity of pointing out to my father how baseless his fears had been. Winter had now arrived and was keeping everybody busy. Every day women brought buckets of coal chips gleaned from the grounds of the Fortress. The men laboured at wedging bits of rag around their window frames; they filled the empty spaces under their wagons with snow and packed it solid so that the wind would not blow underneath. In each of the huge tents they had built a square fireplace of stones, with stacked wood burning day and night so that their best friends – their horses – wintering there, would keep warm and comfortable.

When the young men went to work in the concrete factory, they wore sheepskin, gloves and fur hats with earflaps, and the girls who roamed around the town telling Polish women their fortunes were clad in not one but two flannel skirts and woollen shawls wrapped tightly around their heads. We had food, rationed like everyone else, but were able to supplement it with dried mushrooms, berries, wild garlic and nuts which we had gathered in the forest and stored away for the winter, the way squirrels do. Still, we were never sad – Gypsies rarely are – so there was plenty of music, songs and bursts of laughter floating from the wagons on chilly nights, especially at Christmas time when a big pine tree, decorated with glistening gold and silver tinsel, was set up in the middle of the camp to proclaim our devotion and our fear of God.

On Christmas Day the musicians, dancers and wrestlers boarded a covered army truck to give a performance at the Fortress. Our trio went along – we were now part of the kumpania – and my father, apart from the usual repertoire, ventured into violin solos by Liszt, Brahms and Bartok even though he had only learned the music by ear. When he finished, a tall man, slightly greying at the temples, approached him. There was a glint of vague recognition in the man's round hazel eyes. "Dymitr?" he asked. "Dymitr Mirga?"

My father looked up and shook his head, hardly believing his own eyes. "Count Paszkowski?"

The man smoothed his short, well trimmed moustache, and clapped his hand on Father's shoulder. "Janusz," he said. "To you, Janusz. You remember me?"

"Do I remember you? I haven't seen you for God knows how long."

"I was in Paris. After my father's death. All those years ago."

"And I was in Warsaw. This is my son, Roman."

"My God," Janusz Paszkowski said, shaking my hand. "Time flies. It seems only yesterday that I was challenging you to race me to the highroad. Well, you were always a better horseman."

"A better bareback rider."

"Yes," Count Paszkowski chuckled.

My father glanced towards me. "It's my son's birthday today. The boy is seventeen."

"Oh?" Count Paszkowski turned around and finding a bottle of schnaps on the table, filled three glasses. "Then we must all drink to that." Expansively, he slapped me on the back. I looked at my father, who nodded approval, and raised my glass. "Na zdrowie!" the count said. "To health!"

"Na zdrowie!" we both answered and downed our drinks in one gulp, the way Poles do. The alcohol burned my throat and made my eyes water, but I managed a manly smile.

64

"I promised you a watch for your birthday, Roman," my father said, "but you understand . . ."

"I understand, Father," I said. "It can wait."

"Tell me, Dymitr," Paszkowski turned to my father. "Why did your people move away? Wasn't it comfortable enough on our grounds, on the bank of the Muchawiec River?"

"When your father and you and your mother went to live in Paris, no one in your manor needed our services any longer. So we moved over to the Bug River, closer to town, better income."

"Listen, Dymitr," Count Paszkowski now grabbed my father's shoulders. "Please come to *my* party. On New Year's Eve. You, your wife and son, of course, and maybe two other violinists, and . . ." the Pole raised his head, "where is that girl? She is a wonderful dancer."

"Zoya," I volunteered eagerly.

"Right, Zoya. Just a small group. To entertain us. Like in the old days when my father was alive. Please!"

"Of course we will, gladly," Father answered.

"I shall send a sleigh for you."

"Will you have a kulig?"

"Of course we shall have a kulig." He turned and reached again for the bottle. "Let's have another, eh?" He looked at us and, when I shook my head, filled only two glasses and passed one to my father. "Let's drink to the old times, Dymitr. To the times when we had great New Year's parties, with Gypsy music, followed by a kulig, when sleighs would race each other and the winner would win a kiss from the most beautiful girl. Do you know who that girl will be next week? My daughter. Yes, Dymitr, that's how fast time flies."

It was seven in the evening on New Year's Eve when I heard the jingling of bells and came out of my hut. A man on the high front seat of a sleigh was pulling in the reins to bring his pair of horses to a halt. The Gypsies rushed out of their wagons, eyeing curiously the bewhiskered coachman in his fur-trimmed coat, his legs covered by a sheepskin rug, sitting in his place and staring straight ahead without appearing to notice the greetings of the crowd. Their kinfolk accompanied the musicians and dancers to the carriage, carrying their instruments for them and piling them up in front next to the coachman, in spite of his grumbling and swearing under his frosty breath. The performers ensconced themselves comfortably in the soft seats of the sleigh, tucking their legs under a rug. Then, amidst the shouts of good wishes for a happy New Year, the sleigh turned and we drove away on the crisp snowy path leading out of the Gypsy encampment.

The sky was almost as bright as day, as the bells of the horses' harnesses rang joyfully and mingled with the bells of the sleighs that were carrying town people through this lovely windless night to their own New Year's parties. I raised my face to look at Zoya sitting opposite me, her cheeks flushed from cold and excitement. This was the first time in a month that I had been so close to her. Whenever I passed her in the camp, I would look straight ahead, pretending not to see her, for after my initial rebellion, I had decided that if one lived in the camp and not in Warsaw, then one had to respect Gypsy ways. Still, it was hard to forget our brief encounter by the river, our throwing of pebbles into the water, the glow in the girl's dark, elongated eyes and the small white teeth sparkling between her full lips. I saw her raise her head, conscious of my staring, the skin tightening over her forehead. She turned to my mother and said quickly, "I have never been to a nobleman's mansion. Is it very elegant and rich?"

"Yes," Mother answered. "In the old times when kings ruled Poland, the noblemen used to invite Gypsies to live on their grounds and entertain them during the party and hunting seasons. Not only did we dance for them, our bears danced too." She spoke softly as if telling a fairy tale to a child. "A Gypsy king, Jan Marcinkiewicz, used to be feted

66

by his friend, Prince Stanislaw Radziwill, and often took the prince for a ride in his carriage pulled by six trained bears, with a liveried monkey sitting in the front seat next to a liveried Gypsy coachman."

Zoya smiled dreamily. "I would love to have lived then." She looked up at the wall of barbed wire which surrounded the houses with lit-up windows, purple smoke drifting into the sky from red-brick chimneys. Outside the houses stood the unhitched travelling wagons which the Kelderari had brought with them to the ghetto. Armed German guards patrolled the area.

"Didn't that German colonel press us again to move there?" one of the violinists, Bazyli Tyszko, asked.

"He did," Father answered. "But the Shero Rom answered that our Elders had decided not to abandon our traditional way of life."

"The Kelderari work alongside our boys in the concrete factory."

"The little pay they take home," Father said, "was cut by half. The Germans told them they were deducting the rent for the houses."

"You're a lucky boy, you are under eighteen," Bazyli said to me. "It's hard work in that factory, my son tells me. And you are lucky too," he turned to my father, chuckling, "to be over forty."

There were many people out on the street. Just as on Christmas Eve, the curfew had been lifted for the evening. Boys were returning from skating on the river, with their skates slung over their shoulders. At the sleigh-stand coachmen were trying to keep warm by slapping their arms around their bodies, and women wearing kerchiefs on their heads were hurrying, with freshly baked bread and maize cakes, to the warmth of their homes and festively decorated tables.

Our sleigh, having crossed the bridge, was driving through the deserted, evergreen tree-shaded highroad, leaving the town behind us. The countryside was quiet, except for the clip-clop of horses' hoofs and the jingling of bells. Time and again my eyes rested on Zoya, but she looked steadily at the road, at the trees on either side and the occasional glimmer of lights from peasant huts in the forest.

A quarter of an hour later the horses turned by themselves into a narrow dirt road, driving alongside the River Mucha-wiec. Then the view suddenly opened out and I could see the two-storey white manor house in the distance. Our sleigh entered a large gate, then drove around a rose-bed and halted in front of the servants' entrance to the house. "Here," the coachman said curtly, pointing to the instruments piled next to him, "take them and go through that door. They will call you when you are needed." He didn't even lift a violin to hand it down but just sat there, his undignified mission of transporting Gypsy players and dancers completed.

We entered the kitchen where a white-aproned cook was presiding over a few stout peasant women who were pre-paring food over a huge iron stove. One of them ran to notify the count and a moment later he burst into the room, a glass of vodka in his hand. "Why did that bastard bring you in here?" he boomed angrily. "Dymitr, please come and bring your people along." He put his arm around my father and led him out of the kitchen into a large reception room, where a fire crackled in a fireplace and men and women dressed in faded evening wear chatted in groups, cocktail glasses in their hands. The talk stopped and all faces turned as we made our entrance. The count intro-duced my father to his petite vivacious wife, then snapped at a waiter, "Vodka! Vodka for our guests!" When all the glasses had been filled, Paszkowski raised his own. "Jeszcze Polska nie zginela! Poland is not yet lost!" he exclaimed, quoting the words of the national anthem. We all drank to that. As my father looked around, the count, as if guessing the reason for his scrutiny, said, "No, no Germans here. Not at my party."

"You were at theirs," my father remarked.

"Fodder," the count said. "I supply fodder for their horses. They don't need them for war – no more cavalry charges like in the old times – just for parades. Business," he added. "But it's no business of the Nazis to be in a Polish nobleman's home. And now play, Dymitr. Let the violins play. Soon we shall have dinner, then your performance and the dancing, and at midnight the kulig!"

It was like the old days and yet it was not like the old days. There was no venison or boar meat, nor stuffed pheasants or partridges, nor the potent ruby wine and sweet mead aged in the cellar. The food was the best that the black market could offer – sliced turkey and roast chicken, all varieties of herring and canned sardines and beans mixed with lard, washed down by home-brewed vodka and fruit wine. Throughout the dinner the orchestra played, and then the ladies and gentlemen took their places for the performance and, on a stage improvised for the occasion, my father played his violin and Zoya and my mother danced. Then once again the violinists took over, assisted by my accordion and my mother's tambourine, as the Polish nobility danced mazurkas and obereks among worn-out mahogany sofas and armchairs and brass-ornamented Empire tables, under the dusty chandeliers and the hunting trophies of generations of Paszkowskis displayed on the walls. For that night, for that one night, these people were forgetting that there was no Poland, that in 1939 the Russians had stripped them of their lands and titles, and that the Germans, who attacked the Russians two years later, had kept them in poverty. They were all trying to make their glorious past come alive again in the dawn of the new year, 1943.

At midnight all the glasses were refilled and raised high with a salute and the heartfelt toast for a new era to come and erase all traces of foreign occupation. "And now," Count Paszkowski clapped his hands, "the kulig! Everyone out! The sleighs are waiting!"

Wrapping themselves in their furs, Count Paszkowski's

guests thronged out of the manor and piled into their sleighs. The coachmen, except for the one assigned to us, passed their reins and whips on to the young men and made their way to the kitchen for their share of food and alcohol.

The drivers cracked their whips and, as the row of sleighs moved off, my father rose to his feet with a happy, youthful grin and struck up a tune. We all joined in. The sleighs followed a bumpy country road that led from one nobleman's manor to another, through forests, over fields and meadows and past sleepy villages. Throughout the carnival ride the violins and the sleigh bells merged into a jubilant music that carried the crowd from one mansion to the next, their lights suddenly bright, the servants awake and eager to serve the drinks, and our band playing waltzes, polkas and kujawiaks.

At Count Mirski's house we were welcomed by his eighty-year-old mother, a thick wrap around her shoulders, her cheeks glowing and eyes twinkling. After a dance, when the ladies shouted for us to tell their fortunes, Mother pushed Zoya ahead and, after some hesitation, she gracefully obliged, enjoying the grateful reactions to her predictions for the coming year. Suddenly Count Mirski, a handsome man with a dashing moustache, came up to Zoya, grabbed her hand, and tried to drag her on to the parqueted floor. "Come, Gypsy, dance with me!" Zoya pulled away and I abruptly stopped playing, stepping between the Pole and the frightened girl. "We came here to entertain you, not to dance with you," I said stiffly.

The count pushed me sharply aside and I fell to the floor. He threw his arms around Zoya. "Then give me a kiss. A Gypsy girl's kiss on New Year's Eve brings luck."

Furiously I got back on my feet and lurched forward, clamping my hands on his shoulders. Zoya fled, hiding behind my mother. The music stopped and the couples on the dance floor, bewildered, turned to see what the sudden turmoil was all about. Immediately Count Paszkowski rushed forward and forcibly pulled the Pole away in spite of his protests that a Gypsy had laid his hands on him. "Play, Dymitr!" Paszkowski shouted. "Just play!"

My father started a krakowiak and the couples plunged back into the dance led by the old Countess Mirski as she took hold of her drunken son. The dancing did not last long. "And now – the race!" Paszkowski roared, eager to change the mood. "Back to our manor!"

Outside, the drivers cracked their whips and lashed their horses. The canter soon turned into a gallop. From my seat in a sleigh that tried unsuccessfully to keep up with the racers, I saw the trees merging into one dark wall. The shapes of wooden windmills, village huts and church spires whipped by as the air was filled with the shouts of young men bent forward like Roman gladiators, tugging at the reins, and people in the back seats cheering wildly any time their men overtook another sleigh. Zoya's eyes were wide with enjoyment as she forgot about the incident in Count Mirski's manor. Time and again my father attempted to strike up a tune, but he finally had to give up and sink back into his seat. The jingle of numerous bells was the only accompanying music to the race which finally came to an end when Paszkowski Manor came into view and the leading sleigh stopped at its entrance, a curly-haired man, perhaps barely twenty, pulling his horses to an abrupt halt. Other sleighs, one by one, lined up behind the winner, the horses' manes glistening with sweat, the drivers breathless from their efforts and the rest of the crowd crowing with delight. "Alicia!" Paszkowski cried. "Where is my daughter? I hope she hasn't run off."

"I haven't!" A blonde girl with a pony tail came forward from one of the sleighs. The young man who had won the kulig race jumped eagerly to the ground and planted a hard, noisy kiss on Alicia's mouth. "Hip, hip hurrah!" the crowd yelled their approval.

"Come in!" Paszkowski invited, eager not to let anyone leave yet. "For the last dance."

The guests rushed into the manor, throwing their furs

on to the sofas and even the floor, the men choosing their partners. "Polonaise!" Paszkowski shouted to Dymitr. "Polonaise!" He bowed before his wife and they moved to the head of the row of dancers. And when the orchestra struck the sedate, majestic polonaise, the most national of all Polish dances, the final ritual of the evening began, drawing to a close the joyous night of welcoming in the New Year by the ever-hopeful impoverished Polish gentry.

It was three in the morning when the last sleigh drove away, seen off by the host, our band by his side playing until the last carriage was out of sight. Then with only our sleigh waiting to take us back to our encampment, the count slipped an envelope into my father's pocket and threw his arm around him. "Thank you for coming," he said. "Thank you so much." And perhaps because he, too, was drunk, or merely because he was a Pole, he bestowed a kiss on Father's cheek. "See you soon, my friend."

Only when the horses had passed through the gate and the white manor disappeared from our view, did I dare to look at Zoya. She looked back at me. "Thank you," I heard her whisper.

My mother grinned and my father shook his head in mock reproach. "You're really hot-tempered, my boy," he said, but there was no scolding in his voice, only parental pride.

The sleigh reached the highroad. No other vehicle was in sight. Zoya turned to my mother, hunching her shoulders in girlish excitement. "Tonight it was as if we had all been at the court of Prince Radziwill himself." I glanced uneasily at my father, struck by a strange premonition that this night, instead of being a welcome to the new year, was a farewell to the way of life the Polish nobility had lived for the past one thousand years.

I turned to Zoya. "Did you believe," I asked her, "in what you were foretelling?"

Zoya laughed. "Of course not! But I made them happy, didn't I? Just as your grandmother taught me. Oh, look!"

72

She indicated the full moon and the myriad of stars in the sky. "The Gypsy Carriage." She pointed at the Great Bear constellation, her eyes narrowing superstitiously. "I hope none of its wheels will ever fall. Ever!"

For a while we drove in silence, the horses trotting along the snowy glistening road. I looked around and saw that everyone but Zoya and myself was falling asleep, exhausted from a whole evening's playing. Wide-awake, I watched the sky, the snowfields interspersed by pine forests, the now lightless huts glimpsed amongst the trees. "What a lovely night," I said with a sigh. When no answer came I glanced at Zoya. Her unblinking eyes, darker than usual, were gazing back at me. My heart pined for this ride to last and last for ever, while we sat there, looking at each other, listening to the peaceful clip-clop of the horses and the jingle of bells of the sleigh as it carried us home through the beautiful winter's night of the Polish countryside.

When I woke up, no one else was in the hut. My eyes skimmed over the walls and roof which had been built of old wooden planks and odd pieces of tin. The windows and door had been bought in a junk-yard, the floor was covered with mats and straw for added protection against the cold. The entire furniture of the place consisted of a second-hand cupboard and a table with stools around it. In one corner was a primus stove; pots, jars and canned food stood on a side table, and in the opposite corner there was a bucket and three basins, in accordance with the time-honoured custom, which we Mirgas were obliged to observe: one for the men to wash in, one for the women, and the third for rinsing meat, vegetables and fruit. I washed and then got dressed, deliberately pushing aside the memory of the previous night, which, like the memory of Warsaw, was too painful to dwell on.

When I walked out of the hut, I had to close my eyes momentarily against the glare of the sun, for it was a lovely day, a welcome respite from the terrible winter, God's offering for the holy day of the First of January. At my grandparents' wagon I found my mother serving my father and grandfather chicken and hot broth. Little Mara was standing by her grandmother, watching her bake; the smell of coriander and cumin filled the air. "We didn't want to wake you," Mother said. "Sit down and eat."

I joined the other men and wolfed down the food that my mother put in front of me. Grandfather rose and from a cupboard dug out a bottle and three glasses. He poured out the black drink, his cheeks flushing in anticipation. "I prepared it myself," he said, "from blackberries. It's better than wiśniak. It's a holiday today, isn't it? You, my boy, you are now a man, so you can drink, too." He raised his glass. "To a happy new year," he said. "May the war be over, may the Germans go away and, most of all, may we be allowed to resume our travelling and enjoy the forests, the sparkling rivers and the starry sky over our camp-fires." We clinked our glasses and drank a toast.

Grandmother brought over hot spiced maize cakes, carrying them in her apron. She lingered by the table, awaiting our reaction. When we complimented her by devouring several of the cakes, her tired wrinkled face eased into a broad smile. "I must go now," she said, filling a plate with food, "to take Irina her lunch."

"Give her our best wishes," Mother said. "Tell my sister we can hardly wait until the two weeks are over. And kiss Puji for me." Grandmother wrapped a shawl around her head and left. Two days ago Mother's young sister had had a baby boy in a separate hut built especially for the occasion. Mami, the Gypsy midwife, was allowed to help her, no one else. In that hut she would remain secluded for two weeks, unclean after the birth of her child, unable to be visited, even by her own husband. My grandmother, the camp's Pchuri Daj, was the only one permitted to prepare her food and bring it to her. She reported to the family that the boy was bald and tiny and properly called Puji, a baby bird. What the boy's secret name was even she didn't know;

no one knew but his mother who whispered it into the child's ear – so that there would be two names to confuse the demons who, when angry, would not know whom to curse.

I got up. "I'm going for a walk," I announced, now eager to see the girl I had been so close to the previous night. Zoya's wagon was nearby and I walked towards it. A young Gypsy stripped to the waist, was soaking his chest, arms and face with walnut oil in preparation for the afternoon wrestling match. A mother tried to pull her little girl away from a group of children with a warning that if she didn't come home to wash and eat lunch, a gadje would take her away. In front of Zoya Natkin's wagon sat her seven-year-old brother, Bolek, smoking a pipe and watching his father and two uncles playing a sixty-six-card game. At the sight of Zoya's family I quickened my pace when suddenly a voice stopped me. "Looking for someone?" I turned. The girl's fiancé, Koro, stood at the door of the wagon.

"No, just walking."

"Why don't you race me this afternoon?" Koro said, his face curling into a challenging smile.

"I'm not a very good rider."

"You mean they don't race horses in Warsaw? I hear they even bet on who comes first. I'll give you a thirty-metres head start for a half-kilometre race and bet you one German mark. How about that?"

I shook my head. At the same moment I heard a rustle and Zoya appeared in the door, next to Koro. At the sight of the two of them together my face darkened.

"Then I challenge you to a wrestling match," Koro said cockily, eager for his girl to witness my expected refusal.

"I don't wrestle."

"Oh, no . . ." Koro mimicked me. "But yesterday you were ready to wrestle with a drunken Pole who could barely stand on his two feet. Big hero!" I blinked, but remembered that in a Gypsy camp news spreads fast.

"He defended me," Zoya said.

75

But Koro paid no attention to her. "Remember what I told you when you settled here," he said to me. "And I repeat – stay away from her if you don't want to get hurt!" He stood still, looking at me fiercely and waiting for me to leave. I glanced at Zoya who, after her momentary revolt, fell silent. I turned and walked away.

I wandered amongst the wagons, tents and shanty huts, stopping for a moment to chat with Gregory Mular as he fashioned steel knives and kept the fire going with huge bellows. I passed a row of unhitched travelling wagons, unused during the winter, and out of curiosity halted in front of the shanty of a magerdo who had disgraced himself by eating horseflesh and now had to live isolated from the kumpania until the day that Baro Shero, the Big Head of all the Lowland Gypsies, residing in the Warsaw province, would remove the stigma from him. I meandered along the river, watching the children gliding on it in wooden skates or pulling each other on home-made sleds. When I finally returned home, I heard voices raised inside. The Shero Rom was sitting at the table, his leather whip in his hand, talking animatedly to my father. It was the first time the chief had visited our hut. "Good you returned home," my father said stiffly to me. "The Shero Rom came here with a complaint against you and a demand. And I agree with him. It is our joint decision, Roman, that you must never again talk to Zoya Natkin. If you do, we will have to leave the camp."

"And I will see to it," the Shero Rom added, "that if any of our people are invited to entertain the gadje and make money, my future daughter-in-law stays home. Or you stay home." He got up, clasped my father's hand to seal their agreement, shook it, and walked out of the hut.

There were horse races and wrestling matches in the afternoon and, in the evening, a huge fire was built in the middle of the camp. People brought their own chairs and stools and sat around it. Women carried their babies tied to their waists with huge coloured shawls. We came together with my mother's parents, her brother, Rudolf, who this very afternoon had been declared the wrestling champion of the camp, and her brother-in-law, Leon Kwiatek, a handsome rugged man with a shock of long hair and a round earring in one ear. We all listened to the music of the violins, crying out our longings, our joys and sufferings and then to the cymbals of the same old Gypsy who had played at the Shero Rom's birthday. We heard the men and women chanting their poems, since Gypsy poems are always sung – not once, not twice, but three times so that people will learn them by heart and sing them whenever they feel like singing.

The Shero Rom reclined as usual in his armchair but, this time, on a row of chairs set up next to him, sat his son, his future daughter-in-law, Zoya, and her family. Once or twice I noticed the girl's eyes searching the audience, and I was sure she had also been told never to talk to me.

Leon Kwiatek looked at his wrist-watch and turned to my grandmother. "You'd better go to Irina," he said. "The Sulbotara may come soon." Grandmother nodded and left to set out drink, food and three spoons for the invisible Three Sisters who were due to appear in the newborn's tent on his third night of life, so that they would have some refreshments before whispering into the baby's ear what his future would hold. Two of the fairies would foretell health, happiness and success while the third would prophesy the unhappy moments, since the life of a man is always composed of both good and bad events.

When the music and the singing of poems was over, the ninety-year-old Szura Greczko lit his long clay pipe with an ember, warmed his hands at the fire and then began telling the story of the Gypsies.

"Long, long ago," he said, his pale eyes narrowing as he talked, "the Gypsy nation was the most powerful in the world. Our emperor Pharaoh ruled from Egypt. But at the time there was another great leader, a Jewish general called

77

Moses, and the Gypsy Pharaoh declared war on him and his people. Unfortunately, the Jews then, as now, were better educated and more intelligent than the Gypsies and so they won the war. It is all described in the Bible. When Moses had led all his people out of Egypt and they were unable to cross the big sea because they didn't have ships, he asked his Jewish God for help. And God said, "General Moses, take two sticks and hit the sea with them and it will part for your people." And so Moses did this and his people crossed to the other side of the sea without as much as wetting their feet, while the Gypsy army that pursued them was drowned in the water. But some of our soldiers managed to save themselves and then went into exile; and they, their children and grandchildren began roaming the world, homeless. And that's what I and you, everyone of us now is – a wandering Gypsy."

Old Szura finished his story, but continued to look into the fire, slowly puffing his pipe, contemplating the glorious past. The people around the camp-fire fell silent, wrapped in their own private thoughts, stirred by the passage of the Bible according to the Gypsies.

Suddenly a gust of wind blew across the encampment, rustling the branches of the trees and flapping the canvas of the tents and of the travelling wagons. And with the wind came a flurry of swirling snow. The bitter winter had returned.

5

There was a knock at the door of the shanty hut and we looked up, amazed, because no Gypsy ever knocked before entering. I rushed to the door to open it and saw a lanky Polish boy, about thirteen, standing on the threshold, with a little Gypsy girl behind him. "Are you Dymitr Mirga?" he asked, looking at my father. My mother and sister were out.

"Yes."

The boy turned round and spoke to the girl. "I am at the right place, you may go now." Reluctantly, the girl left, throwing an enquiring glance over her shoulder.

The boy closed the door. "Someone wants to see you urgently," he said.

"Who?"

"He didn't tell me his name. He's waiting on the main road. He asked me to be as discreet as possible. Please come."

My father looked at me, bewildered. "I'll come with you," I said.

As we walked quickly along the tree-shaded path leading out of the encampment, the Polish boy said, "I was just passing by when this man halted the sleigh, snapped his fingers at me and gave me half a mark to call you."

I looked at the road we were approaching and saw the familiar sleigh with the coachman sitting in front, reins in hand, and Count Paszkowski, covered by a fur rug, in the back seat. We had not seen the count for well over two months. "Another party," Father said, smiling with anticipation. As we approached the sleigh, the boy left.

"Hello, Dymitr," the count said, hurriedly. "Get in! You, too," he added, glancing at me. "Drive there into that side road," he ordered his coachman. He kept silent, his face troubled, until the sleigh had driven some hundred metres. "Turn in here, behind these railway trucks." The sleigh stopped in a deserted goods depot.

"Dymitr," the count said. "I came here straight from the Fortress the moment I heard the news. To warn you. Tomorrow morning the Germans are going to surround your camp and requisition your horses. I know how important the horses are to you. If they do requisition them, you will no longer be able to travel."

Painfully, my father closed his eyes and drew a deep sigh. "Or run away if we have to."

"Yes," Janusz Paszkowski repeated, his voice sinking, "and run away if you have to. A German soldier came to my house on a motorcycle with a message that I must deliver enough fodder tomorrow for one hundred horses. I drove to the Fortress right away. I don't have that much fodder. I would have to buy it from the peasants. So I asked for money, because I don't have any, and I got it. And in the Fortress I learned, don't ask me how, what they plan to do. They are also taking the horses away from the Gypsies who live in the ghetto. I thought, Dymitr, that perhaps you could leave at once. It's already the ninth of March. So you could start your travelling season a bit earlier than usual, even if it's still cold. But not a word, remember, to anyone. I'm sticking my neck out for you."

My father clasped the count's gloved hands and shook them in gratitude. "Thank you, Janusz, thank you very much. Not a word, I promise. Not a word. And we'll leave by night, on side roads." It was the first time since the two men had met again, after years of not seeing each other, that my father had called his boyhood friend by his first name.

80

"And now you'd better return to your camp and start packing up," Paszkowski said. "I'd rather you walked home from here. I'll wait." I saw my father's arms lifting to embrace the count. "Go," the count said. "Don't waste any time."

Father and I jumped quickly from the sleigh and walked back as fast as we could. We crossed the highroad, then rushed over the path to the camp and made straight for the wagon of the Shero Rom.

Father burst through the door first. Mikita Kowal was not there. Koro was sitting on his bed, whittling a wooden ladle with his knife. "Where is the Shero Rom?"

The boy lifted his head, looking not at my father, but at me standing behind him. "In town, on business. What's the matter?"

"When will he be back?"

"He said at five."

Exasperated, my father rubbed his face. "Tell him I must see him urgently. If he comes back before, I'll be at my home. It affects us all, all of us in the camp."

"I will tell him."

We left. "What shall we do?" I asked. "It's two and a half hours."

"We can do nothing without him. Let's go home."

We reached our hut, but neither Mother nor Mara were back yet, so we walked over to my grandparents' wagon. My mother and grandmother were sitting, darning their men's socks. Mara was combing her doll. My grandfather was wrapping black tobacco in a piece of newspaper. "I have something important to tell you," Father said. "Mara, go and play outside." The girl looked up, startled, but obediently picked up her doll and left. The women stopped darning their socks and looked at my father's worried face. "The Germans are going to surround our camp and take all our horses. Tomorrow morning," Father announced.

"How do you know?" Grandfather asked, nervously blinking his eyes.

81

Father hesitated, but only for a moment. "I promised the person who warned me not to involve him. If the Germans found out, he would pay dearly for it. I will tell you, but remember, no one else, not even Wala's parents, must know where the information came from." And then he told them.

My grandfather put away tobacco and newspaper, no longer wanting a smoke. He sat down heavily on a stool. "I have one old horse," he said, his shoulders sagging, his voice low and forlorn, "but it took me and Rosa all over the country. When we ate, he ate, and when we drank, he drank."

"It's more than just losing horses, Father. Once they get them, we are stuck. They can come here any time and round us all up. We must leave at once, tonight. By morning, when the Germans get here, we'll be far away."

Grandmother nodded, deep in thought. "You must go to the Shero Rom at once."

"He won't be back till five. I'll see him then. And meanwhile start packing."

Grandmother burst into uneasy laughter, showing her few crooked yellow teeth. "What's there to pack? It will take us half an hour to gather together all we need to take with us."

It was shortly before five when I saw Mikita Kowal walking towards the camp, dressed in a fur jacket, fur hat and top boots. I rushed forward. "My father wants to see you. It's urgent."

The Shero Rom threw me a cold look. "Then let him come to me. I receive people in my wagon. I don't go to them."

"It's a matter of extreme importance, my father said. To you and to all of us."

"Oh, all right." Mikita went ahead and pushed the door of our hut open. At the sight of the Shero Rom, my mother took Mara by the hand and quickly left the men alone.

"What is it?" Mikita asked, sitting down. "Have you something to drink, something strong?" He smiled. "I made a good business deal, I need a drink." Father poured him a glass of wiśniak and he downed it with one gulp. "Well, I'm listening."

"I learned that the Germans are going to take our horses. Tomorrow morning."

"Eh?" Mikita looked at him, incredulously. "How do you know?"

"I can't tell you, but I can swear on the Holy Bible that it's true. I'm ready to take a candle oath or even a cemetery oath if you want me to. This time you must believe me. You have two horses yourselves. Once you lose them, once all our horses are taken, we won't be able to run away if we have to." My father talked feverishly, anxious to convey the urgency to the Shero Rom.

"Calm down, Dymitr," Mikita said. "And sit down. Sit, I said. We have to reason everything out calmly."

"For God's sake," Father burst out, almost angrily. "Can't you see the writing on the wall? First our horses, then us, in a few weeks' time perhaps, when we won't any longer be able to escape. That's what they are after."

"All right, all right . . . Look, you tried to scare us before. Three months ago. And what happened? Nothing! Gossip, rumour, that's what it was and that's what it is now. How can I, I who am responsible for all of us, evaluate your information if you refuse to tell me where it came from?"

"My God!" my father cried out. "What does it take to put some sense into your head?"

Indignantly, Mikita rose to his feet. "You know to whom you are talking?"

"I know. A stubborn Gypsy, for whom it is more important to prove that he is right than to safeguard his people." My father gestured at the Shero Rom. "I'm going to call for an urgent meeting of the Elders."

"Only I can call such a meeting. And they can only advise, nothing more. I decide. And it is my decision that unless you tell me who told you this stupid piece of gossip, I'm not going to pay any heed to it. And now I'll go to see my friend, Colonel Krüger, and ask him straight to his face. He won't lie to me."

"Don't you dare!" my father exploded. "If you do, they will surround our camp immediately. Roman, go and get the Elders at once."

Mikita smiled. "The Elders will listen to me, not to you. As they have before. All right, Dymitr, I won't go to the Fortress if you are afraid. I wouldn't want anyway to tell the colonel that a man of mine has reported a silly piece of gossip. Since you arrived here from Warsaw and asked us to run away immediately, time has proven me right, not you. You want to hear once more that the Elders support me? All right, I'll let you have that pleasure. Go to them, call them together for a meeting." He walked to the cupboard, poured himself another drink, drank it, and left.

"I will fetch the Elders myself," Father said. "Starting with my father." He threw the door open. I saw my mother and sister outside, both looking at the Shero Rom as he passed them by.

"He doesn't believe you?" Mother asked.

"No, a stubborn, stupid Gypsy!" Father rushed into his parents' wagon. A few moments later I saw his tall figure reappearing through the wagon door. "Come here, Roman!" I went up to my father. "We must warn the Kelderari!"

"What for? It's too dangerous." I heard my grandfather's voice, then saw him taking a few steps towards us. "It will be enough of a problem just for us to leave. The more people who know, the greater the danger will be of the Germans pursuing us. What do you care about the Kelderari anyway?"

"They are Gypsies, aren't they? Roman!" Father paid no attention to Grandfather's warning. "Go to town towards the ghetto. When you see a Kelderari outside, any

Kelderari, tell him to warn their chief, Dombrowski. But don't you dare enter the ghetto, remember!"

"I won't," I said. "I'll go right away." I returned to my hut, told Mother what Father had ordered me to do, put on my coat and left.

Within minutes I had reached the highroad, then turned right, walking fast, anxious to get back to the camp as soon as possible. The sun was setting and I felt a cold gust of wind on my face. From time to time I blew into my hands because I had forgotten my gloves. There was hardly any traffic on the road. Suddenly I noticed far ahead a wooden barricade thrown across the street, with a few Germans manning it. It had never been there before. I could make out a soldier checking the documents of a Polish man and a boy, refusing to let them pass and waving them on to a side street. My eyes darted to my right. Liberty Park started nearby and I dashed towards the fence. Making sure no one had seen me, I ripped out one of the wooden planks, got inside the park and elbowed my way through dense foliage on to a path. The park was completely deserted. After a ten-minute run I reached the park's entrance gate, far behind the barricade and close to the ghetto.

No Germans were on the street, not even any Polish people. I crossed the road and threw myself into the shadow of the two-storeyed houses flanking Jagello Street. Clinging close to the wall, I reached the point where the barbed wire veered away from the main road into a side street. There was still about half a kilometre to the entrance of the ghetto, but I hoped I would find somebody on the other side of the wire, call him, and pass the message on to him. In the dusk I could just see the ghetto houses in front of me, their doors and windows ajar, pieces of cardboard and clothing strewn over the ground, blowing about in the wind. There was no smoke coming from the red brick chimneys. A few mongrel dogs roamed around.

With my heart pounding, I continued to creep along the

85

barbed wire, searching for some sign of human life. There wasn't any. A storm seemed to have passed through the place, sweeping everyone away with it. Suddenly I heard a distant neighing and after a while the view of a cobblestone square inside the ghetto opened up to me and I saw a big tent there. Through the flapping canvas entrance I could see horses inside. And then the terrible truth dawned on me. The Germans had taken the Gypsies and left their horses behind!

"Hey!" I heard and instinctively started to run. "Stop, you silly boy!" The words were Polish. A young woman was standing in the doorway of her house and beckoning to me. "Come here, quickly!" I hurried back. "You – escaped?" she asked, shivering from the cold. "Come inside the house, quick!"

I slipped into the warm room and the woman closed the door behind me. An acetylene lamp hanging on the wall threw an eerie light over an old woman with tin-framed glasses, spinning yarn on a spinning wheel. She looked up at me with hostility and fear. "You'd better get rid of them fast, Zofia," she muttered.

"All right, all right. Isn't there one drop of compassion left in you, Mother?"

I turned to the young woman. She had a round rosy face and a severe bun. "What does she mean? Is there anyone else here?"

"It's all right!" the woman said loudly, speaking across the door leading to a room inside the house. "You can come out! It's another Gypsy." Slowly the door rattled open and a swarthy, high-cheeked face appeared in it. It belonged to a tall boy about my own age.

"You are not a Kelderari," the Gypsy said in a dialect slightly different from what I was used to.

"No, I'm from the camp near the Bug River. What has happened? For God's sake, tell me what has happened to your people!"

The boy now slid out of hiding. He wore bulky trousers

86

and a jacket with silver buttons. "They took them all . . . The Germans."

"When?"

"Just an hour ago."

My whole body went limp with terror. "My God! How?"

"Shortly after the trucks brought the young men home from the factory, they came back, this time full of German soldiers. A number of other trucks followed and halted outside the gate. Some of the soldiers surrounded the ghetto, while the others broke in, burst into the houses and began shoving the people out with their rifle butts. They left us no time to pack. Our children cried, our women screamed. I managed to hide in an attic and from there I could hear a German officer trying to calm the people down, telling my father that this was just a resettlement, that they would also be taking all of you away tomorrow, and that we all would then be moved to another place to live and work."

"Resettlement!" I sneered. "That means a concentration camp."

"My father didn't believe them either. I heard him say in our language for me not to come out. When it became quiet, I slipped out of hiding, ran across the deserted streets of the ghetto and managed to sneak out under the barbed wire." He showed me his arm, streaked with scratches and blood.

"Get rid of them both, please!" cried the old woman to her daughter. "Do you want them to take us away too?"

"Who is your father?" I asked.

"Dombrowski," the boy answered. "I'm the son of the chief of Kelderari."

"Will you stop chatting away in that devilish language of yours and get out!"

The younger woman glanced at her mother. "You'd better go," she said to us with a sigh. "It's dark now. You will manage to get out of town."

"Come with me to our camp," I said. "We shall be leaving immediately, I'm sure. You can go with us."

"Are you sure that will be all right?" the boy asked. "I am a Kelderari."

"You are a Gypsy, aren't you?"

"All right, let's go. We're not welcome here anyway." He extended his hand. "I am Pawel Dombrowski," he said. And suddenly, unable to hold back his pent-up emotions, he burst into tears. But a moment later he bit his lips and wiped his eyes. "Let's go."

I turned to the younger woman. "Thank you, Pani Zofia," I said.

She led us to the door. Outside it was completely dark and we scurried down the street, running fast towards Liberty Park. The curfew was now in force.

We crossed the park and at its end struggled through the wooded area towards the surrounding fence. I easily found the same spot where I had broken in. I pushed Pawel out first, then followed him. I grabbed his hand and we went on running. When we reached the camp, I led the Kelderari boy straight to the tent where the Elders were holding their meeting. I could see the flickering light of an acetylene lamp coming from it and hear raised voices. I burst inside through the canvas door, pulling Pawel along with me.

The hum of voices abruptly ceased. All the faces, including those of Mikita Kowal and my father, turned towards us. "They have taken them all!" I blurted out. "All the Kelderari. An hour ago. Only he, the son of their chief, Dombrowski, managed to escape."

"My God!" I heard my father shout. "It's even worse than I thought." He moved, almost viciously, towards the Shero Rom. "Do you – do you need any further proof that I was right?"

Mikita Kowal, speechless, looked around the terror-stricken faces of the Elders – suddenly a broken man, no longer the self-assured leader of the camp. Gregory Mular jumped to his feet. "We no longer have time to talk," he

88

said. He clenched his fist and shook it at Mikita. "You were wrong all along. And I said so three months ago. But you, too," he turned to the Elders, "none of you believed Dymitr. Do you believe him now?" He paused, waiting. No one said a word, not even the Shero Rom. "We must run," Gregory went on, "while there is still time. Whether the Shero Rom agrees or not."

Mikita Kowal raised his head in a last attempt. "Tell us, Dombrowski, tell us what happened." Pawel Dombrowski told them what he had told me. Then he added, "The Germans don't have enough trucks. They are all at the front. So today they took us, tomorrow they take you. And then the same trucks, as they have no other vehicles, will return, and bring the horses to the Fortress. I know their arrangements, I heard that officer tell it to my father."

Gregory Mular, who had remained standing, spoke again, raising his voice. "I now ask you, the Council of Elders, to choose a new Shero Rom. Yes!" he bellowed. "A man capable of leading us out of this mortal danger threatening us all, the only man who has foreseen this day. Dymitr Mirga!"

Suddenly the howl of a dog outside the tent broke through all other sounds and all the dogs of the camp immediately joined in. "You heard that?" my grandfather cried from his seat. "Gypsy dogs don't howl unless the danger is real."

"What are we waiting for?" Franko Zbar asked sarcastically. "For the owls to hoot also? They will – if we remain here."

Szura Greczko got to his feet. "I am the oldest here and I say we leave at once, and I say Dymitr Mirga is our new leader. Please accept, Dymitr."

"You can't!" Mikita Kowal rose from his chair, trying to oppose the move. "You have selected me as your leader for life."

"In unusual circumstances we can change our leader,"

old Szura said. "In unusual circumstances we stop advising, we decide. This is our unwritten law. I'm now putting the matter to a vote. Please raise your hands, Elders, if you want Dymitr Mirga to become our new Shero Rom." The eight hands of the Elders shot up. "Dymitr Mirga," Szura continued, "do you accept our call to become our leader?"

"I do," my father answered firmly. "I accept."

"You are our new Shero Rom," Szura Greczko announced. "Take your rightful place at the table."

His teeth clenched in anger, Mikita Kowal left the table and walked out of the tent. My father now took the Shero Rom's place. He turned to the Elders. "There is no time for me to make acceptance speeches," he said. "I am honoured and I'll do my best to save us all. Now go to your wagons and gather the things you'll need for the journey." He pulled out his watch. "It is half past six. At seven thirty you must all be ready, all the horses harnessed to our travelling wagons, all the things you need packed, and we'll start. We have a night, a whole long winter's night to get as far away from here as possible."

Zenon Cysin got up. "Which road shall we take?"

Pensively, my father rubbed his face. "We cannot go through the town," he said. "People will see our caravan heading south."

"Also there is a German barricade now on the main road," I added.

"And we cannot go east. East is the Fortress."

"So we must go north," Franko Zbar said. "It's the only road left to us. It will not lead us abroad, but it's the only way to get out."

"You're wrong," my father said. "We can't take any of the highroads. If we do, the Germans will find us in no time."

"So how shall we escape?"

"West."

"West is the river."

"The river is frozen," my father said. "Our wagons will

cross it, then find a country road leading south. It won't occur to the Germans that we crossed it. In one hour, not later than an hour, I want to see you in your travelling wagons and ready to move. Spread the word."

Word spread fast. The Gypsy women quickly packed their few family belongings and carried them to their canvas-covered wagons, while the men led their horses from the big tent towards the river and harnessed them, and then brought enough sacks of fodder for their animals to last for several days. The dogs had stopped howling long ago, and children now tied them to the axles, so they could run alongside the wagons.

My grandmother put her china, her pots and all the food she had into a sack, and all the family pictures and that of the Black Madonna, together with her and her husband's clothing into an old battered valise. My mother gathered the family belongings – leaving half the things scattered behind – for the second time in a few months. She dressed Mara and herself warmly and saw to it that my father and I were well prepared for the journey. We both put on long underpants, coarse flannel undershirts under our suits, overcoats and top boots. On my father's order I went around the camp, telling people to keep their voices low even though we were far from the main road. I saw Koro harnessing two horses to his wagon; he gave me a look, full of hatred. I helped whomever I could to carry their things to their wagons, harness their horses, and tie up their dogs. I saw to it that Pawel Dombrowski was allocated a place on the cart carrying the unmarried brothers of Wala, to be driven by Rudolf. I noticed that the Natkins were left to fend for themselves, with Zoya struggling hard to help her parents, and I deliberately went to help her, disregarding Mikita Kowal's order to stay away. He no longer was my Shero Rom, his orders were no longer valid. And Koro was not even there. He was worrying about himself and his father, preparing their two horses to drive the two of them, and not even offering to take some of his fiancée's folk or their belongings into his practically empty travelling wagon. Finally, I lent a hand to Gregory Mular, dragging his bellows to his cart. When I returned, I saw him gathering up his ironwork, which he hoped to sell on the road. "Can I buy a knife from you?" I asked.

Gregory picked up a long, fancily chiselled knife. "Against the enemy, eh?" he asked. "If the need arises."

"Yes," I answered. "If the need arises." And I pushed the knife down the top of my right boot. "How much?"

"Nothing. A cousin of mine and the son of the Shero Rom pays me nothing."

"Thank you."

It was time to move. Women carried their babies in their shawls tied to their waists, pulled their small children by their hands and settled themselves inside the wagons under their canvas roofs. Leon Kwiatek helped his wife up to her seat, carrying his baby in his arms. Even the magerdo, who had eaten horse meat and been isolated from the rest of the kumpania, had been forgiven by the new Shero Rom because of the unusual circumstances, and he also was busy helping his family to prepare for the journey. All the Natkins were in their cart by now and all of us piled into my grandfather's wagon, with me holding the reins for my father.

Snow began to fall – the soft, white flakes floating through the air. Father raised his eyes heavenwards. "The snow will cover our tracks," he exclaimed. Grandmother pulled out the picture of the Black Madonna, kissed it and kept it close to her large bosom.

My father sent two men to check that no one had been left behind. He himself ran between the wagons until he spotted my uncle, Rudolf. "We start crossing the river right now," he declared. "You go the other way, over the path, and then drive a hundred metres or so over the highroad in the opposite direction. Be sure no one sees you. On your way drop some clothing and some pots to the ground, to mislead the Germans, so that they will think we are heading north." He rushed to some neighbouring wagons and returned with a few house utensils. "Here are some more things you can leave strewn on the road."

"All right," Rudolf Puma smiled. "It's an order, Shero Rom." He smacked his lips at his horse, lashed at him with the whip, and turned the cart around.

My father mounted our wagon. "Don't rush!" he shouted, his standing figure seen by everybody. "Keep in line – one wagon at a time, so we don't break the ice. Go!" he motioned to the Natkins' cart. He watched their horse carefully slide down the embankment then, when their wagon had reached the middle of the river, he waved the next cart to start. By the time most of the wagons were on the other side of the Bug, my uncle had returned from his mission. "I did as you ordered, Shero Rom."

"Good. Thank you, Rudolf."

It was shortly after eight, when only one cart remained on this side of the river, that my father finally took the reins from me. "Viooo!" he spurred the horse on. And the horse, who had taken my grandparents all through Poland, eagerly crossed the Bug to the other side, where all the wagons were already waiting. My father drove past them and took up his position in the front of the caravan, as its leader.

The wagons rolled through a vast snowfield, with hardly any trees or brushwood around, their sole aim to get as far as possible away from the camp. The white curtain of falling snow made us feel secure and calm. In his seat my father was leaning forward, trying to penetrate the white darkness in front of him, so that the caravan would not miss any country road that we might come upon. My grandfather breathed a deep sigh. "I'm sorry, son," he muttered in a broken voice. "I said I knew better than you, because I was a wise old man, but I was wrong, son. I was really just a silly old man – that's what I was."

My father waved his hands. "Never mind, you meant

93

well." He kept straining his eyes. "I think there is a road," he said. "Can you see?"

"Yes," I said. "It's completely covered by snow, but it's definitely a road."

The moment our wagon reached the road, my father turned left. "We shall be riding parallel to the Bug River," he said. He raised his eyes, and though he could not see the sky, not even a single star, his lips moved in a prayer.

I looked back and saw Bora Natkin, his swarthy face damp with snow, wheeling his cart round too. I could not see Zoya, but I could imagine her sitting inside the covered wagon with her mother and small brother, silent and frightened.

There was a flicker of light to our right. We were passing a hamlet, a hundred metres away, a window of one of its huts lit by a dim kerosene lamp twinkling in the darkness. "We are heading towards Włodawa," Grandfather said from behind. "Fifty kilometres from here."

"Good," Father said.

"I don't know these roads too well. I know the ones on the left bank of the Bug better."

"So do I," my father said. "I haven't forgotten."

We came to a crossroads with a wooden figure of Christ nailed to a cross. The snowfall slackened; we could now see the trees and hedges on both sides and the view of an ancient Polish cemetery looming in front of us. "Give me some straw," my father said, turning. "There is plenty on the floor." Grandfather handed him a fistful and father tied several stalks together. "I must leave spéra," he said. "In case some of the Kelderari have escaped. Here!" He handed a straw-band to me. I jumped down from the cart and fastened it to the cross, its narrower side pointing towards Włodawa, so that other Gypsies could read the sign and know this was a safe road to take.

The other carts followed us along the narrow road, shadowed by rows of snow-covered poplars, shimmering in the pale moonlight and the wash of the stars. The muffled

94

thud of horses' hoofs and the squeaking rattle of iron wheels were the only sounds that accompanied the caravan. I looked over my shoulder. My grandparents, my mother and sister, her doll in her arms, were all dozing, exhausted, their bodies swaying with the movement of the cart.

"You'd better take a nap, too," my father said. "We'll have to double as drivers."

I wrapped myself more tightly into my coat and let my head fall over my chest. In no time I had lapsed into an uneasy, fitful slumber. As time went by, the cold became more bitter and the night darker. It was midnight when my father's voice woke me. "Here! We stop here. The horses must rest."

In the wide clearing of the forest the wagons pulled up one next to another. The men got up, carrying sacks of fodder to feed their animals. Several heads of the families gathered around my father. "We are about thirty-five kilometres from Brest Litovsk," he said reassuringly. "We won't stay here long. As soon as our horses have finished eating we must move on."

"Where are we going?" Zenon Cysin asked.

"Hungary," my father answered. "Six hundred kilometres."

"You think we can manage it?"

"With God's help," my father replied, "we will make it. It's a free country. There are no Nazis there. And a hundred thousand Gypsies, twice as many as in Poland. Roman! I want you to count all the wagons, horses and people. As you come to each wagon, ask how many people it carries. And write it all down. Have you got a piece of paper and pencil?"

"I have, Father." I went around. "How many are here?" I asked Zoya's father, trying to sneak a glance inside the wagon.

"Four," Bora Natkin answered. He was a curly-haired, moustached man in his forties. "All asleep."

I went on. When I returned to my father, I reported,

95

"Twenty-seven wagons, thirty-five horses, eighty-four people."

"Get in," he said. He then raised his voice. "Get back to your wagons! We are moving on!"

My father slapped the reins. He drove back to the road over a narrow bumpy forest path, the other wagons falling into line behind us. The caravan turned south again. "Here," he said to me, "take the reins," and a minute later he was fast asleep in his seat.

I managed to make myself remain wide-awake, the responsibility of leading the caravan weighing heavily on my shoulders. As the road twisted and turned, I glanced at the sky to see what I had learned in my distant Gypsy childhood. The Great Bear, the Gypsy Carriage as we called it, was north, so driving away from it meant I was on the right track. I led the column until my father woke up three hours later to take over the reins from me again. Occasionally we passed a scattering of huts and barns with thatched roofs, a church spire or a wooden windmill. When the outlines of brick houses appeared in the distance, Father swerved his wagon away from the road.

"What are you doing?" cried a voice from the Natkins' cart.

"We must by-pass Włodawa," Father answered. Once more we drove through a field, no longer hidden by the falling snow. The ground was frozen and hard and the horses, rested and well-fed, broke into a fast trot. Once the town was behind us to our right, my father again searched for a country road. When at last he found one, he smiled with relief.

More and more clusters of trees were looming on both sides and dawn was beginning to break, a pearly light mingling with secret blues drifting across the snowfield, the trees and our road. Then, out of the shadows of the morning, a big pine forest appeared, becoming more distinct as we came near to it, the branches heavy with snow, the needles green and unchanged by the frost. We found a path and Father turned into it, glancing over his shoulder to make sure that the others followed him. Half a kilometre away from the road, deep in the forest, was a large clearing. One after another, the wagons drew up, making a circle the way they always did during their travels around Poland.

Father rose. "Here," he shouted so that all could hear him, "we shall remain for the day, and we shall continue the journey when night falls." Exhausted, but glad, he jumped down to the ground. All the wagons, all his people were safe. I looked at him with pride, and then I pressed my lips tight with satisfaction and a warm feeling of accomplishment. In the past ten hours I had grown from a shy Warsaw schoolboy into a man. I thought gleefully of our camp, a long winter's night and sixty kilometres away, where the German officers would by now be reporting to Colonel Krüger that his Gypsy friends had managed to outwit the Nazis and escape.

6

We slept in our wagon, huddled together, deriving what warmth we could from our furs and blankets, and from each other. Outside, the wind whistled, making the canvas flap and stirring the branches of the trees.

I was the first to waken; I crawled to the front of the cart and leaped to the ground. I looked up at the sky and from the position of the hazy sun knew that it was already late afternoon. Most of the people were still asleep, but a few of the men were trying to rekindle last night's fires and checking on their horses, their rumps covered by blankets, the tall wagons encircling them for added protection from the frost and wind. Some slept standing, as horses do, the others ate oats from sacks hung over their necks or drank melted snow water from buckets. The odours of animal urine and excrement permeated the area. I poked the ashes with my boot until I found a few glowing embers, then brought some dry twigs from the wagon. I soon had the new fire going and filled a cauldron, hanging from a trivet of sticks, with snow. By the time the rest of my family had dragged themselves out of the wagon, the water was boiling. The women then took over, throwing in fistfuls of wheat and oats. "Ask Pawel to share our food," my mother said to me. "He has no one now. Let him always eat with us. Is it all right, Dymitr?"

My father nodded. "Of course."

I went over to Pawel and extended my mother's invitation to him. The boy's face broke into a grateful smile and he immediately walked back with me to my family.

The camp now came alive as other men lit their fires, attended to their animals and began whispering in groups as though afraid that people passing on the road half a kilometre away could hear them. Leaning against our carts, we all ate, making one meal out of last night's supper and this morning's breakfast. Mikita and his son kept to themselves. The former Shero Rom was used to having the camp women cook for him, but now no one volunteered to help him. Koro opened a can of beans and offered it to his father, but he waved it away, unhungry and sulking, his dark deep-set eyes, blood-shot from a sleepless night, occasionally staring fixedly at the Gypsies with the wounded expression of a man betrayed by his people.

My father crawled into the wagon to check that all our musical instruments had been safely brought along. After a few minutes he crept out again into the open. "I think," he said to my grandfather, "it would be a good idea to send someone to find out where we are and where the Germans are."

Grandfather shook his head. "It's better not to call the wolf out of the forest," he said. "We ought to cross the river back to the east anyway."

"Yes, but not until we get far enough from Brest Litovsk. We must scout the area, we don't know this part of Poland at all."

Suddenly the horses began neighing and the dogs howling furiously at the sky. A moment later we heard a thunderous noise above our heads and then saw a formation of Stuka bombers, black crosses visible on their fuselage, passing over and disappearing into the low cloud. As the sound of their engines faded in the distance the animals calmed down.

"Let *me* go, Father," I said. "I don't look Gypsy. I have a Warsaw overcoat. I need only trim my hair a bit. I will take a horse and ride to the nearest farm, or maybe I'll meet someone on the road."

For a moment my father hesitated, but I was already in

the wagon, looking for scissors. When I crawled out with them, I said to my mother, "Cut my hair." She looked at my father. He nodded his approval. Ten minutes later I was ready.

I made my way to the road, then continued forward, not spurring my horse too much so as not to tire it, but finally, noticing a cart being driven by a thick-bodied peasant, I pulled up alongside. "Praised be Jesus Christ," I greeted him.

"For ever and ever," the peasant answered, eyeing me.

"Returning from market?"

"No, just visited my sister in Rudki. Do you know Rudki?"

I nodded. "Yes, I do."

"I haven't seen you around. You sound like a towns-man."

"I'm from Włodawa. No doubt you have Germans here like we do?"

The peasant slapped his reins, but his horse refused to speed up. "Plenty. If you ride with me, you'll see a lot of them. In Sobibor."

"It must be a small village. I never heard the name."

The peasant laughed. "A small village, a big camp. Four fences of barbed wire, and a deep ravine and a minefield all around. At least a hundred thousand Jews are there. And Gypsies. Lights burning all night, you can see them from my village."

"Gypsies? Are they taking them as well?"

"Yes. Only yesterday I saw truckloads of them. You should have heard them screaming and wailing."

I suddenly became aware of a sharp, heavy, smouldering stench in the air. I looked up and saw a huge tongue of smoke rising up in the eerie red sky. "What's burning there?" I asked.

"People," the peasant answered. "The Germans gas them, throw their bodies into pits, soak them with gasoline and burn them." My whole body went limp and my stomach turned cold. "But not before they strip them of

100

gold fillings and women's hair," the Pole went on. "Every night, a freight car carries Jewish and Gypsy clothing, shoes, hair and gold to Germany. Have you got a cigarette?"

"No," I said, feeling sicker by the minute. "I don't smoke. Well. I must get back. Praised be Jesus Christ."

"For ever and ever."

"Viooo!" I turned my horse and snapped the reins, spurring it to go fast. My heart was pounding as never before. Fearful of encountering some German soldiers, I galloped back to the forest where my people were waiting. When my horse and I, both perspiring heavily, reached the clearing, I jumped to the ground, forgetting to tie my animal, and ran to our wagon, past my mother chatting by a fire with Pawel Dombrowski and two of her brothers. My father was sitting inside the cart, rolling cigarettes out of a newspaper and black tobacco for himself and for my grandfather. "We are heading straight for an extermination camp!" I burst out.

Father sat up with a start. "How do you know?"

"I saw it. A huge flame and a column of smoke. A Polish peasant told me they burn Jews and Gypsies there." I lowered my voice to a whisper, conscious of Pawel's presence outside the cart. "From what he said, I believe they brought the Kelderari to that place."

Father shuddered. "Don't tell anyone," he said, his voice cracking. "Let us not spread any panic. Go around and tell people that, as soon as it's dark, we shall be crossing the river to the east. Say we know the roads and forests there and many villages which have been friendly to us in the past." Grandfather nodded his approval.

I rushed out, caught my horse and brought it back. Pawel approached me. "What did you find out?" he asked.

"That we shall be better off on the other side of the Bug. A Pole told me there are many Germans around here."

"Did he see any trucks with Gypsies, by chance?"

"No," I said, swallowing hard.

Pawel rubbed his eyes. "I'll probably never find out

where they took my people." I remained silent, but as I was harnessing my horse to the cart, I could not erase from my mind the image of the huge flame and the bluish column of smoke rising up into the winter sky.

An hour later we were travelling again. Our route lay across a vast stretch of land sparsely covered with shrubs, shielded from view by the dark night. The wagons moved in a line, horse following horse out of habit, the only sounds the crunching of wheels over the crisp snow and the occasional cracking of whips. Then a few kilometres to the north came the rumble of a passing train. Was it a German troop transport going to the front, or was it a train carrying the condemned to Sobibor or taking their useful remains – gold fillings, hair, clothing – back to Germany? The thoughts, the unwanted thoughts, kept gnawing at my mind, as I prayed next to my father who, I knew, was also praying that the Bug River would soon appear in front of us. The wind began to blow harder, right into our faces. After an hour of riding, we still saw no river. We reached a pine forest. The snow started to fall heavily from the leaden clouds that hung low, wrapping the night sky in a blanket of grey. It became harder to move along the rough path among the trees, and the horses, blinded by snow and wind, slowed down. The dogs began whining in fright.

It took us two more hours to traverse a stretch of forest only three kilometres wide and then to emerge from it, with the hazy view of a hamlet just in front of us. But behind the huts, where the flickering lights were still burning, we could see at last the winding course of the river.

Once more my father tried to direct his horse away from the road so that the caravan would avoid the village, but the animal refused to budge. I leaped from the cart, grabbed the horse's bridle and led it to the side. Immediately, both my legs and the horse's legs sank knee-deep into the snow. The horse snorted, extricated himself violently and climbed back on to the road. My father and I exchanged fearful glances. "We have no choice but to go through the village," he said. "Maybe they won't notice us in the snowstorm."

A small cemetery, with a white church, loomed up in front of us, and then, some hundred metres later, a cluster of thatched huts and sheds appeared, flanking the road. When we reached the middle of the village, with a well in its central square and a chained bucket clattering on the ground, I saw a face flattened against a window-pane. A moment later the door was flung open and an old white-haired peasant stood on the threshold. He cupped his palms around his mouth so that we could hear him above the roaring wind. "Where are you going, Gypsies?"

"Across the river!" Father answered, his voice edged with fear. "Any Germans here?"

"No!" the man shouted. "Three kilometres to the south, at the bridge, but not in Stawki. Go with God!"

"Thank you, good man!"

I saw the Pole shake his head in sorrow, then go indoors again and slam the door against the fury of the storm.

As we approached the Bug, my father halted the caravan. He passed the word along that we must get rid of our dogs. There was no other way; they could easily betray our presence as we travelled and also during our night camps. A few of the men gathered, protesting, and the one who protested most was Mikita Kowal, although he had no dog of his own. But my father stood firm. He ordered the owners of the dogs to tie their animals to the trees. In the morning, he added, the villagers would undoubtedly let the dogs free.

To ease the horses' burden, the men walked alongside their carts, guiding the animals by their bridles down the river. Then the crossing began – one cart at a time so as not to break the ice. The dogs began to whine when they saw that they could not follow their masters; the children cried at being abruptly deprived of their pets, but the desolate cries of both the dogs and the children were drowned by the shrieking wind. It was another hour before all the wagons managed to get across to the other side in the whirling, blinding snowstorm. Somewhere in front of us wolves began to howl. Behind me my grandfather was muttering to himself the age-old Gypsy complaint, "Are there only wolves left in the world, no people?"

We crossed the river, then the highroad from Brest Litovsk on which only yesterday the Kelderari had probably been driven to their deaths. The horses plodded through the frozen marshes of the Pripet River that almost reached the Bug. "We are in the Ukraine now," Grandfather said. "I know the area. Soon we shall hit a track going south."

It was midnight when we found it; but by then the storm had turned into a veritable blizzard, the wind strong enough to scoop up huge clusters of hard snow from the fields and hurl them against the wagons. I walked beside the horse as it lumbered ahead at a snail's pace, peering desperately ahead to find some wooded area where our caravan could shelter. All around us there was nothing but vast emptiness, except for an occasional leafless roadside tree.

"A spéra!" I heard my grandfather's cry from the wagon. "On that beech. Pick it up!" I plucked a little bone wedged under the tree bark. "Four Gypsy carts passed this way," Grandfather said, pointing to four grooves in the bone. "Put it back now – for others to read."

"The horses won't be able to go much further!" I yelled.

"We will stop as soon as we can," my father answered.

Suddenly I saw Pawel's figure emerging from behind the curtain of snow. He grabbed our horse by its bridle on the other side and for a while we both managed to trudge on, pulling the horse ahead. The freezing flurries of rain and snow were lashing my face, and my legs were feeling heavier by the minute. But then my horse stopped and refused to move further. My father leaped down, but neither his, nor mine, nor Pawel's shouts, nor the whip, persuaded the animal to budge. My grandfather then clambered down from the cart. Gently he patted the perspiring horse's snout, whispered softly into its ear and, amazingly, the animal, recognising the familiar voice of its master, started again. The other horses followed suit. Pawel grinned happily at me and then walked back to join his own cart.

Suddenly we saw lights flickering in the distance. "It's a village!" Father called. "Let's hope a friendly one. We have no choice but to stop there."

But as the caravan, plagued by the swirling snow, plodded on, the lights seemed to remain as far away as before, like ghosts teasing people to ride on and on until they were completely exhausted. Then the lights disappeared altogether behind the clouds of snow, but just when my father was about to order the wagons to stop and form a circle, one single gleaming light reappeared, this time much closer. A short time later I cried out, almost with joy, "I see a house!" A wooden thatched hut loomed up some fifty metres in front of us. The column halted. My father and I pushed forward, heads lowered against the wind and snow, but at that very moment the lights in the hut went out. "They have gone to bed," Father said. "Look!" He pointed to his right. There was a small cluster of trees there, large enough perhaps to shelter the caravan.

"What does it mean?" I asked, looking at the door of the hut.

My father joined me. There, on the front door of the house, was a circle carved in the wood. "Good village," he said. Then he looked closer. "There is a dot in the circle. A *very* good village! I can still read the spéra," he smiled. "We will camp in that wood," he said, almost jubilantly. "I wonder who the Gypsies were who preceded us, but whoever they were – our people, or the Kelderari, or the Lowari – they deserve our thanks."

"Look." I pointed at the hazy outlines of some other huts further away.

"Yes. Tomorrow we will go into the village and buy

some supplies. We need bread, oats, and milk for the babies."

We hurried back to the caravan. It was impossible even to shriek the orders because of the roar of the storm, so we both went around and informed the men that we were halting in the wooded area and that the village we had come across was a friendly one. "I know it," my grandfather said. "It's called Horodnice. They have always welcomed Gypsy ironsmiths, always had work waiting for us."

"Good," Gregory Mular said as he and the other Elders gathered around their Shero Rom. "We will make some money from the gadje."

As the wagons moved as far into the wood as they could, I noticed strange blurred contours among the trees, then made out what they were – Eastern Orthodox crosses. The wood was the village's cemetery!

We parked our vehicles as much in a circle as was possible, with the horses as usual inside. We threw blankets over their backs and fastened them, then we fed them, and let them drink the snow. We were much too exhausted to start fires to melt it. I walked over to the Natkins' cart. "Do you need any help?" I asked.

"Thank you," Bora Natkin answered. "We can manage."

"Thank you, Roman." I heard a shy whisper from inside the wagon, though I could not see Zoya's face. Her burly father and her very young, slim, olive-skinned mother looked at their daughter, then at me and, then, wonderingly at each other.

In spite of everything – the blizzard, the war and the Nazi persecution – I felt elated as I lay down in my wagon, exhausted but unable to sleep. I had the feeling, the unmistakable feeling of the young, that the girl cared for me and that, while everyone else was looking to the next day with fear, I was awaiting it with joy, because it would bring more glimpses of the girl riding in the cart behind me. My entire body ached, but I was getting used to the toil and pain of the journey. Then I felt a small body pushing close to me. It was my little sister, Mara, trying to wedge herself between me and my mother, for warmth and comfort. For a while I kept stirring where I lay, but at last my thoughts went blank, and I fell into a bottomless well of deep sleep, no longer conscious of the outside world, of the howling wind and driving snow engulfing the Gypsy caravan, of the village sleeping peacefully through the blizzard, or of the strange, cruel war in which soldiers killed not only soldiers but whole peoples.

We slept until the late hours of the morning. By then the storm had spent itself. With flints we lit fires between the gravestones and began to prepare meals. My father was already gathering together a group to accompany him into the village, including myself and my grandfather. "I think you'd better ask Mikita to come along," Grandfather said. "He dealt with the local peasants when he was our Shero Rom."

My father walked over to Kowal. "Please come along with us," he said. "You know the Horodnice people."

Slowly the stocky man raised his head, the skin tautened on his face. "You lead the men!" he snapped. "Show us what you can do in a village where you have to arrange work for them, and not in a night where you can fiddle your way through."

Father shook his head, angered, but did not answer. We returned to my grandfather. "It's no use," he said.

The group selected for the foray into the village continued their preparations. The men expected to return with some orders for blacksmith work. The old women filled their little sacks with medicinal herbs and good-luck amulets, the young ones shoved packs of cards into their bodices; they hoped to be able to barter their medicinal help and promises of good fortune for food. The winter sun came out from behind the clouds and we felt unafraid and confident as we walked straight into Horodnice.

107

The village was alive with people shovelling snow away from their doors, attending to their livestock, women feeding their chickens, the older men sitting on benches, smoking clay pipes and chatting as if waiting there for the spring that was just around the corner. But as we strode into the single street of Horodnice, I noticed how the people stared at us, shaking their heads to themselves. The women suddenly began chasing their children into the houses, and then they and their menfolk walked away, back into their homes. Even the old people stopped chatting, abandoned their benches and scurried indoors. Dogs began to bark viciously at us. My father, bewildered, motioned the others to stop. "What is happening?"

"I know a peasant who lives over there," Grandfather said, pointing to a small dilapidated hut, smoke coming out of its clay chimney. He knocked at the door. Like all the Gypsies of Brest Litovsk, he spoke Ukrainian. "Hey, Kola!" he shouted. "We want to buy food from you. Buy, you understand? To pay good money! Do you hear?" He heard no answer and pressed against the door. It was bolted. "For God's sake, Kola, what's going on here?"

Finally we heard the key turn in the lock and part of the bearded face of an old man appeared. "Go away, Gypsies!" the peasant muttered, alarm in his voice. "Don't bring us any more misery."

"What are you talking about?" My father pushed his foot forward to stop the peasant from closing the door.

"Germans came this morning. And the Ukrainian police. Because of the terrible snowstorm we sheltered four Lowari families here. They not only took them away in their trucks, but also arrested the men in whose houses the Gypsies slept. Run away, Sandu, and hide for your own sake!" With all his strength the man pushed away Father's leg and bolted his door.

My heart sank. I looked at my father. All the others, too, looked at their Shero Rom, panic visible in their faces. "Let's get back to the wagons, quickly," he ordered, and

108

our entire group, like a flock of scared birds, scampered back to the encampment as fast as we could.

Just as we reached it, my father saw a man's pockmarked face in the window of the hut that stood outside the village, opposite the cemetery. We rushed towards it, but the peasant's face vanished instantly. "Which way did the German trucks go?" Father yelled to the unseen man inside the house.

A voice answered, "Towards Lukov. That's where they came from. They have troops, a police station and a prison there."

"Is there any forest nearby?"

"Yes," the answer came again. "A huge one, three kilometres down the road. On the way to Lukov."

"How far is Lukov?"

"Six kilometres. Go now, please, for God's sake! They are probably back in Lukov by now. Get to that forest and God have mercy on your souls. And I swear to the Almighty God, I won't tell anyone you went there."

"Bless you," Grandfather said.

Our entire band hurried back to the wagons. The news spread fast among those who remained behind. Even Mikita Kowal was stunned. Women began to whimper and babies to cry. "We must get to the forest immediately," Father ordered. "It is the only chance we have."

"And they are supposed to be good people?" Grandmother snorted. She spat on to the ground and swore under her breath. "One of them must have informed the Germans. That's why they came."

A short time later, with our wagon leading the way, the caravan started again. We went straight through the village, because there was no other way to go, and because my father wanted to make sure that the villagers knew we were leaving the area. The street was still deserted; only in the windows did some women appear, a few of them making the sign of the cross after us. My grandmother leaned forward, so that they could see her, and responded with the same gestures of blessing, while her pale lips moved in an avalanche of curses on the inhabitants of Horodnice, blaming them all, all the gadje, for the misfortunes of the Gypsies.

Once we had left the village, we lashed our horses forward in a desperate effort to cover the open road between the huts and the forest as fast as possible. Time and again my father looked over his shoulder to make sure that no informer passed us by. Horodnice, fortunately, like all small Ukrainian villages, had no telephone.

"I can see it!" I shouted. "The forest." I was young, I had the best eyes. Father hit his horse hard with his whip. He was not sorry for the animal – it was a matter of life and death.

The forest proved to be a huge one, the way the peasant had described it. Almost immediately we found a bumpy path that led into the trees. The caravan turned on to it and soon was engulfed by pine trees, their branches glistening with snow. I uttered a great sigh of relief. My face was damp; my entire body was drenched with sweat.

The wagons drove on and on, but suddenly the path ended as it approached a small crumbling hut. "Probably a forester's cottage," Father said. "It appears to be abandoned."

The wagons quickly drew in all around the house. Bora Natkin broke the hut's locked door. Except for a rusty iron bed, a table and two stools, a few dirty pots and a stack of dried wood, the place was empty.

People climbed down from their carts and with the wood found in the hut, they lit low fires, so that the smoke should not be visible outside the forest. "God protects those who protect themselves," Grandfather muttered. Slowly our tenseness dissipated. We were at least a kilometre from the road and felt safe, although both we and our horses were still hungry and thirsty. Tomorrow seemed a long time off. We went about our chores of preparing a meal, even exchanged some forced jokes and laughed the way people

110

do who feel relieved of the danger facing them. Once more we had managed to escape the Nazis. How much luckier we were than the Kelderari and that little caravan of four families which had preceded us on the road to Lukov.

It was early in the afternoon when Jan Michalak, the wrestler, who, incredibly at this time, was doing push-ups in the snow, suddenly halted in the middle of his exercise.

"Did you hear that?" he asked, raising his head, then getting to his feet.

"What?" people around him asked.

"Trucks! I can hear trucks rumbling from the side opposite to where we came."

We strained our ears. The sound of engines became more pronounced. "There must be a road there," my father said. "Perhaps the one from Lukov, which skirts the forest?" We now heard not only the rumble of engines, but also faint German voices. Then suddenly the motors were shut off. The distant barking of military commands could be heard. We held our breath, frozen in our places. "They have stopped on the road," Father said after a long pause.

I made up my mind. I was not going to ask my father for permission. I decided to edge towards the area from which the voices came. If the danger became real, if the Germans started combing the forest, I would run back to warn the others. Summoning my courage, I started to walk slowly away from the wagons, so that no one would suspect my plan, but Pawel Dombrowski followed me. "I'm coming with you," I heard him say, his tone brooking no opposition.

We walked a few hundred metres, the German voices growing louder by the minute, and then, unmistakably, they were joined by the cries and the wailing of women. Pawel stopped and motioned to me to proceed very carefully, dashing from tree to tree, making no noise at all, avoiding the branches. As we almost reached the edge of the forest, a view of the road opened up in front of us. Canvas-covered trucks stood there, preceded by an open half-track, a German officer in black uniform standing in it, with a death's-head on his black cap, and next to him a soldier manning a machine-gun. Several other soldiers were on the ground, their bayoneted rifles pointed at some Gypsy men who were shovelling snow from a large ditch into which it had fallen during the night. No women were in sight. Unable to comprehend what the men were doing, I remained glued to the tree, a few metres from Pawel. The work continued. The snow on the banks of the ditch grew, the men seemed to sink deeper and deeper until only their faces could be seen.

Suddenly the officer shouted, "Halt!" He motioned to the soldiers. They formed a line and went up to the ditch, then raised their rifles. The officer lifted his hand and abruptly brought it down. A salvo of rifle shots broke the air. From my drawn lips came a stifled cry of pain and fright. I realised, to my horror, that the men had been digging their own common grave. Most of them, felled by the bullets, disappeared from view, but I could see a few Gypsies, probably only wounded or some who had managed to avoid the bullets, pull themselves out of the ditch with savage effort and begin running towards an open field. The machine-gun went to work, mowing down every man who tried to escape.

Again I heard that horrible wailing and then I saw the Gypsy women with their babies being pushed out of the trucks with rifle butts by civilians who had been guarding them. The guards jumped after them in order to assist the soldiers. My throat tightened as I watched the screaming and cursing women, many of them throwing themselves at their oppressors, clawing their faces and tearing their hair. They were hit by rifle butts or booted down, and then shoved ahead until they, too, slid into the ditch. Those who, in their rage, spat at the Nazis and their Ukrainian helpers, had their babies wrested from them and, in front of their mothers' eyes, the babies' heads were smashed against the tree trunks. Blood spattered all around. The children's bodies were thrown into the ditch. As the lamentation and cries for mercy got louder, the SS officer impatiently gestured to the machine-gunner who lowered his fire directly into the ditch. The screaming ceased almost immediately and then the firing stopped. No one remained alive. Rigid with horror, I was unable to move from the spot. I turned to Pawel and saw my friend's face drained of all colour.

Now the Ukrainian civilians picked up the shovels left by the Gypsies and pushed all the snow that had previously been scooped out of the ditch back into it, burying the dead. The officer ordered his men and the militiamen back into the lorries. The Germans and the Ukrainians climbed in. The engines started. All three vehicles turned right around and then rumbled back towards Lukov, leaving no trace behind of the execution.

Only when the sound had faded into the distance did I recover my voice. I had never seen, nor could have imagined, anything so horrible. I walked over to Pawel, who was weeping. "This is what they probably did to my family," I heard him mutter through sobs.

"Stop crying!" I said harshly, though my heart went out to my friend. "We must get back and tell my father what we have seen."

"They will get us, too," Pawel went on. "They will get us. We are all doomed."

No one in the camp had even noticed our absence. They had all heard the lamentation and the screams of the dying. I went to my father, took him aside and told him what I had seen. His eyes blinked nervously as he tried to live up to his role of the Shero Rom, and make a decision. He could not do so. Finally, he said, his voice breaking, "I'm sure they were the Lowari they took away this morning. They probably questioned them in Lukov about any other groups that might be on the road or hiding in forests, and then brought them here, far away from the town and people.

113

I suppose they don't bother to send small groups to extermination camps."

He walked on a few steps. His face as always remained haggard but then, as he stopped by a tree, all by himself, he was unable any longer to control himself. For the first time in my life I saw my father cry. For his family, for himself, for his people.

The winter sun was setting when suddenly we heard a noise coming from the depth of the forest. Just like earlier in the day, we froze in our places and listened. "Probably some animals," my father said. "Deer or wolves."

"No," Grandfather said. The old man's hearing was better than that of many a younger man. "Those are boots. People, not animals."

Once more panic struck the encampment. The sound of advancing steps and the crunching of snow could now be heard more distinctly. A number of people dashed towards their Shero Rom, their eyes pleading for a quick decision. Women and children began to weep. "We are done for," my grandmother said almost calmly. "It's now our turn to die." My mother held a string of beads in her hand, whispering Paternosters and Ave Marias.

Slowly, methodically, the heavy tread of studded boots and the sound of cloth brushing against pine branches were coming nearer, and now could be heard also at the opposite side of the encampment. Finally my father found words. "They are surrounding us!" A few Gypsies fled into the woods. The clicking of rifle bolts sounded very close. Father crossed himself, but did not move. There was little chance of escape and, as long as most of his people remained in the camp, their leader would not run away. Like the captain of a sinking ship, he would remain. My mother lifted her sobbing daughter into her arms, as if her mother's embrace could save the child. At this moment of terror, when most of the people thought of themselves or their families, I found myself searching for Zoya. She was very close by, standing by her cart together with her family. I walked over to her and, without saying anything, took her hand. She turned her face to me, her eyes a wet blur, but kept her hand firmly in mine.

Suddenly from amongst the trees all around us emerged men, their rifles at the ready. They were not soldiers, but wore civilian clothes. Ukrainians, I thought. The same who helped the Germans to execute the Gypsies. My eyes darted around. We were surrounded by perhaps thirty armed men. I had no doubt that we would all be shot by a fusillade of rifle bullets, and the final, helpless thought crossed my mind that I was going to die before I had even had a chance to live or to kiss a girl. I squeezed Zoya's hand as hard as I could as we waited close by each other, our hands clenched, unmindful of her family, or my family, or her fiancé – waiting to be shot together.

Suddenly we heard, not the crack of rifle fire but laughter, loud, raucous laughter that spread from one armed man to another. "The devil!" I heard a yell in unmistakable Polish. "They are not Germans, they are Gypsies!" They lowered their rifles. Their leader stepped forward. "Don't be afraid of us!" he shouted. "We are partisans. We are not your enemies! . . . Who is in charge here?"

As he advanced towards us, we joined the Poles in a laughter of sheer relief. Those who had fled into the forest came back. "I am the head of the group," my father said, moving forward.

The two men, the Polish and Gypsy leaders, met in the middle of the camp. The Pole extended his hand. "I am Captain Jan Lipinski," he said.

Gratefully, my father clasped the man's hand. "Dymitr Mirga."

The Polish officer shook his head in bewilderment. "How long have you been in this forest?"

"Since this morning."

"You know that the Germans and their Ukrainian collaborators, led by Stefan Bandera, having finished with the

115

Jews, are now killing Gypsies?" My father nodded. "Where did you come from?"

"Brest Litovsk. We travelled at night and hid by day."

"You must be mad! In Gypsy wagons, in Gypsy dress! God Himself must have protected you. It's a miracle you were able to get this far. Where the hell are you trying to get to?"

"Hungary – where there are no Germans."

The officer wiped his face. He paused, thinking hard, then he said, "You must not go any further. That is, if you want to stay alive. Have you any food?"

"Some, not much. Probably enough for a week or two."

"Good. By that time the snow will have melted and the spring come. We have orders to move then to the other side of the Bug. You are Gypsies, but you are also Poles. As long as we stay here we shall protect you. But then you will be on your own."

"Thank you, sir."

The Gypsies and the Polish partisans all now surged towards each other, shaking hands, joyfully exchanging slaps on the back and chatting together happily.

"Get rid of your Gypsy dress and the canvas covers of your carts," the Polish officer said to my father. "Trim your hair and change your clothing. And, for God's sake, break up your caravan and go in small groups, a few wagons at a time. During daytime. Pretend you are peasants going to market, or riding home."

"It's good of you, sir," my father said. Then he added, "Tonight we shall hold a feast in your honour. We shall light fires, cook, and sing and dance for you. That is, if it is safe?"

"It's safe. At night it is safe. We might as well enjoy one night. Still, keep your music and your voices low."

"We shall," Father said. And then he startled the Polish officer by grabbing his shoulders and giving him two smacking kisses, on each cheek, the way Polish men do.

116

7

It was a most propitious day for the Gypsies to move on. Not only had a pair of bats flown over the encampment throughout the night but, when the morning dawned, a magpie circled over, chattering endlessly as if urging us on. "Luck is with us," my grandfather said. "Let's get going."

It was early April. Winter had passed, the mud caused by the melting snow had dried and the spring was in full bloom. The Polish partisans had left the day before, having provided us with food and clothing bought with our gold in the friendly Polish villages that were interspersed among the Ukrainian ones – for the Western Ukraine had belonged to Poland for almost two decades before World War II. The previous evening all canvas covers had been taken off the wagons, all the embellishments and good luck amulets removed, the wheels and horse harnesses stripped of their silver and copper ornaments, and all Gypsy clothing discarded. Everything was gathered into piles, which were then set alight. The fires were kept low to prevent the smoke reaching above the trees and betraying our presence. What remained after the fires died down was buried in the ground.

As the day arrived, with all its brightness, my father said, "We are ready to go." He looked around with satisfaction. Everyone was dressed like a Polish peasant; men wore peaked caps on their heads, the women babushkas. Their hair was trimmed, their jewellery hidden. The carts looked like regular village carts. We were going to travel, a few carts at a time, separated by long intervals. And at the day's end we would gather in a big forest familiar to all of us. There the Shero Rom would take a count of his people. There was one thing which my father could not alter – the faces, the swarthy Gypsy faces. But then there were swarthy peasants, too. Throughout history Tartars and Cossacks had invaded this land and left their imprints on later generations of Poles and Ukrainians.

It was six o'clock when the first three carts began their journey. As usual I was sitting next to my father, both because of my fair features and because from time to time I would take over the reins. As we started along the forest path to the road, I was intensely aware that the most dangerous stage of our journey would be the first one. Even if we managed to find the side road skirting Lukov, we would still be passing only about half a kilometre away from the town harbouring the Nazis and their Ukrainian collaborators. An hour later we found ourselves beyond Lukov, with some German soldiers encountered on the road who paid no attention to us, and some Ukrainian peasants greeting us with "Slava Bohu" – "Glory to God" – as they passed by. With all my heart I hoped that the same luck would hold for the other groups that were to follow us. My grandfather had no such fears. The omens were just too good to be afraid of anything. Apparently he was right, for we drove safely along on lonely winding tracks, past small villages, past peasants sowing in the fields and the scarecrows they had erected, past holy images in their silver settings with oil lamps burning eternally beneath them.

Occasionally I turned my head to glance at Zoya riding in the cart behind me – my view no longer obstructed by the canvas cover – and to enjoy the flutter of eyelashes and the cheerful twinkling of her dark eyes. It was no more than had happened during the past two weeks, but in the camp I was always conscious of the presence of others, still uncertain how to handle the new situation, just basking in the happiness of loving and being loved, with no one but the two of us sharing our secret.

I looked at my father. He was grinning to himself, secure and unafraid. I felt as if his youth, all his spring-summer-and-autumn travelling youth had come back to him. The lovely road that usually curved out of sight, shadowed by tall poplars and silver birches, the pine forests, and the rivers encountered on the way which flowed into the Bug – all reminded him of how much he had missed during his years in the city. My father was a Gypsy at heart and nothing could change that, not even the fact that our carts no longer looked like Gypsy ones. It was almost as if he had forgotten about the danger, as if the war and persecutions had never happened, as if the clock had turned back to the late 1920s.

The trees were now all covered with young, light green leaves, the birds had returned, and over our heads flew noisy flocks of starlings, bustards and blue jays. But the loveliest sight of all that our eyes feasted on was that of wild flowers popping up everywhere and colouring the fields – yellow dandelions, blue forget-me-nots, cornflowers and red poppies, around which the bees were buzzing. "Drom romano!" I heard my father say, heaving in a big sigh of the spring-scented air, "The Gypsy road!" A string of wild ducks rose from a dale and flew over us, flapping their wings, happy and free. My father looked up, following their flight.

"All right, son," he said, handing me the reins. "Drive! Learn what it means not to be confined to four walls, to be at one with nature, its smells, its sounds, its colours, everything that the gadje miss. Learn again, my boy, to feel free. Like those wild ducks!"

We arrived at our destination, not far from the town of Vladimir Volynskij, late in the afternoon, and drove deep into the forest until we reached the clearing close to the stream where we had arranged to meet. We made tents

119

from blankets over trivets of sticks, mindful to keep them off the paths, because Beng, the devil, liked to stroll over them at night. An hour later the next four carts led by Gregory Mular arrived, and half an hour after that another three carts headed by Franko Zbar. It looked as if the other groups were also making their journey safely.

The horses were fed and watered, children sent to collect mushrooms and berries, women began cooking soup from potatoes and nettles, and men settled down at the stream with their fishing rods. Darkness fell as we began our dinner of fried fish with mushrooms, following it with a dessert of blackberries and roasted acorns. Most of the carts had arrived by now and the people, exhausted from their trip, were preparing to retire. They took heart from the day's journey that had gone so well. The fields and forests provided them with food; the earth, carpeted by grass and pine needles, gave them the softest bed in the world; the night sky full of bright stars was balm to their eyes. What more did a Gypsy need? In addition, this was the night of the new moon. The old men, led by Szura Greczko, turned to it, bowed and whispered their prayers. "T'e avel bach-telo a son nevo" – "Let the new moon bring us happiness." "Amen," the old women chimed in fervently, fingering their rosaries.

I lay on my back, unable to sleep, listening to the even breathing of the members of my family. The last two groups of carts had still not arrived, but I did not worry about them for, led by Zenon Cysin and Tomasz Klimko, they were not due until midnight. I could not sleep, because the night was beautiful and I was acutely aware of the Natkins' tent close to ours. Restlessly, I got up and walked between the trees towards the stream. Suddenly I stopped. My heart skipped a beat. Zoya was not in her tent. She was right here, leaning against a tree, watching the reflection of the new moon in the water. "Zoya!" I whispered. Immediately she turned to me.

I ran to her. Shutting her eyes, she fell into my arms.

Recklessly, I lifted her head and brushed my face against hers until my mouth found her eager, parted lips. With a stifled cry, she wrapped her arms around my back, hugging me to herself with all her strength. We were making up for the long wait of all the years of growing up and of those almost unbearable two weeks in the encampment since we had confessed our love for each other. Finally I managed to tear myself away for a moment, gently lowered her to the ground, and then lay next to her on the grass, her ear close, inviting endearments and confessions; but all I could do was to murmur her name over and over again and kiss her hair, her forehead, her neck and then find her mouth again, sweet with her youth and the forest berries. With a sigh, her head slid down on to my chest, her heavy-lidded eyes still shut. "I have never kissed anyone before you," she whispered.

"Neither have I, Zoya," I confessed.

"I have loved you, Roman. Always!" she went on, her fingers clutching me, talking rapidly as if time was running out on her and she had to say all that had been on her mind for so long. "Every Christmas when you returned to the camp, I suffered, oh God, how I suffered. I thought we had lost you to the big city, to Warsaw, and I tried to find solace in my engagement to Koro. My parents and his father arranged it, without ever asking me. But I would rather die than marry Koro!"

"Shh!" I lifted her head, looking straight into her eyes which, as I gazed at her, finally opened, almond-shaped and misty. Then her mouth tightened as she hugged me ardently again and whispered, "Take me, Roman, please!"

"No!"

"Take me! Don't you understand?" Her face was flushed, almost feverish. "If I am yours, they can do nothing. They can't keep us apart, they must marry us. They can't change the Gypsy ways."

"No!" I repeated. "I don't want it that way."

Her skin tautened over her face. She stopped listening.

121

She grabbed my face, sank her mouth into mine, making my head whirl, and then again thrust her body against me, twisting her long legs around mine and her arms around my neck, drawing me to herself, brooking no resistance, because she knew I could not resist. A violent shiver went through me, my hands helplessly darting into her blouse, grasping her small up-tilted breasts, making her utter cries of pleasure. Then my body swung over hers and I fell on top of her. She cried out my name and moaned. But suddenly I heard a rustling of leaves and heavy footsteps approaching. I slid away from the girl and looked up. In front of me stood Koro. In the light of the stars and the moon, I saw the boy's face filled with hatred, his hands moving to the top of his boot. A steel blade glistened.

I jumped to my feet. Zoya shrieked and backed away. "I told you," Koro said through clenched teeth, "to keep away from her. But you didn't and now you'll pay for it!" He pounced at me, ready to thrust the knife into my chest, but I managed at the last moment to dodge, and the blade only tore my sleeve and grazed my arm. We turned quickly to face each other. "You'll not come out of this alive!" Koro snarled, raising his knife again.

With eyes focused on him, my hand darted to the top of my boot. I whipped out my knife. "I'm not afraid of you!" I snapped back.

As Zoya covered her mouth with her hand and whimpered, we began stalking each other, knives in our hands. Then I jumped and succeeded in kicking him in the groin. He doubled up in pain, but his hand still held the knife. "You son of a crow!" he yelled and then hatefully turned to Zoya. "And you – a whore! Don't think I didn't see it. I saw it all! You deserve each other. You can have him – dead!"

Suddenly from behind the trees emerged Pawel Dombrowski. "Are you both crazy?" he shouted. "Just at the time when our lives are in danger, all you can do is to fight each other!"

"He drew his knife first," I said.

"A Gypsy trying to knife a Gypsy will be declared a magerdo. Is that what you want, Koro?"

"He is not a Gypsy, he is a gadje!"

"He is the son of the Shero Rom," Pawel answered.

It was like rubbing salt into Koro's open wound. Once more he lunged, trying to stab me. Zoya cried out with fright, but once again I dodged the assault and grabbed Koro's hand. With our faces close to each other, filled with hatred, it now became a contest of strength. I had no idea what power Zoya's love had given me until this very moment, until I finally forced Koro to unclench his fist, letting the knife fall on to the ground. Pawel dashed forward and grabbed it. Koro backed away a few steps, then blurted out, "All right, go ahead, kill me!"

We heard footsteps. Through the trees emerged several men, awakened by the noise of our fighting. I slipped my knife back into my boot. "It was Koro who attacked him," Pawel said, showing Koro's knife. Koro walked away, head bent, past my father, the new Shero Rom, past his own father, the former Shero Rom, and disappeared from view.

"Magerdo!" someone shouted. It was Gregory Mular, his eyes following Koro into the woods.

Father rubbed his face with his hand. "Forget all this," he said. "Forget it. All of you! We have much more important things to worry about. The next to last group has been caught near Toropino and wiped out, executed on the spot. Our men in the last caravan saw the carts overturned near the road and eleven bodies sprawled around them. Zenon Cysin, Zdenko Grabowski, Jan Michalak . . ." His voice choked and for a moment he could not continue. Then he caught his breath. "They are all dead. And who knows how many of us will survive tomorrow? Go to sleep now, all of you. There is a long day ahead of us."

Mikita Kowal, his face full of anger and hatred, took a step towards me and raised his fist as if about to strike, but then veered round and, instead, lashed at my father with a barrage of words, trying to stop the people already leaving the area. "You are responsible for their death, Dymitr!" he shouted. "You wouldn't let me go to Colonel Krüger to check your piece of bloody gossip about the Germans taking our horses. We would have stayed. I could have arranged things with the colonel. But, no, you had to scare our people into running away. They were safe there – there, not here on the road!"

"Didn't the Nazis take the Kelderari? Didn't they shoot the group of Lowari near Lukov?"

Mikita waved his hand madly. "Kelderari, Lowari! What are they to do with us?" He turned and faced his entire audience. "You should have had faith in my friendship with the Germans – then nothing, I repeat nothing, would have happened to us. A Gypsy leader has to be wily and shrewd to deal with the gadje, and for fifteen years I did well for you, until that bareforytka Roma – what am I saying, he is not even a Roma – until that gadje," he pointed at my father, "came along. It is his fault that our men died today!" He spat on the ground, and walked away.

My father looked around at the people. "I wouldn't pay any attention to him," the paunchy Franko Zbar said. "None of us does any more."

"But he may be dangerous," Gregory Mular warned. "We had better watch him. He may go to the Germans and ask them to take us home. Or denounce us, to save his own skin and his son's. Who knows? I don't trust him."

My father shrugged. "Let us not exaggerate," he said, but I saw him gazing worriedly after Mikita. He paid no attention to me, showed no relief that I had come through the fight alive, nor any feeling at the sight of Zoya bandaging my bleeding arm with a piece of cloth she had torn from her own skirt. He was my father, but not only my father. He was the head of the Lowland Gypsies of Brest Litovsk, responsible for them all.

8

We travelled on, always taking small dirt roads, a few carts at a time, gathering each evening at a pre-arranged spot deep in the forest to take count. All along my father saw to it that spéra were left – a rag tied to a branch of a telegraph pole, a bone wedged under a tree bark, a broom left on the ground – signs to his people and to any other Gypsies to follow us this was a safe road. The three following days were uneventful, but on the fourth a group of three carts never arrived. No one knew what had happened; the people had simply disappeared.

It was the day after, in the afternoon, that my father abruptly pulled in his reins. "God!" he said, his face stricken with horror. In a ditch by the road were sprawled the bodies of a man, a woman and two children. "Our people, the Lowland Gypsies," my grandfather said, judging the dead by their attire.

"We must bury them," my father said. "Pick up the shovels." Speechless, I looked at the dead, the imprint of terror in their eyes, the entire family wiped out, their bodies laid near the road, a warning to others, a testimony to history.

Suddenly from behind a cluster of trees emerged a cart driven by two grey oxen, a few men riding on it. As it approached us a white-bearded Eastern Orthodox priest jumped to the ground. "Who are you?" he asked. "Poles – or people like them?" My father remained silent, so we kept silent, too. "We came to bury them. Gypsies or no Gypsies, human beings not dogs . . . Who are you?"

"People like them," my father answered. "We also wanted to bury them."

"Then come with us."

We placed the bodies on the cart and then the funeral procession started, headed by the priest carrying a black flag and a cross, and a diminutive short-bearded dyak, the church singer, chanting Ukrainian songs for the dead. We and the peasants walked behind.

We came to a small poplar-shaded cemetery at the entry to a village. A row of four fresh graves had been dug in the earth. We laid the bodies next to them. The Ukrainians spread thick towels over the chests of the dead Gypsies and placed loaves of bread on them, so that they would have food on their celestial journey. My grandfather pulled out a bottle of home-made blackberry liqueur from his coat pocket and sprinkled drops of it over the dead, to add a touch of Gypsy ceremony to the Ukrainian one. The bodies were lowered into the graves. We shovelled earth down upon them. As our women clasped their hands over their heads, crying out their sorrow, the dyak's funeral song rose to a crescendo. The priest said a prayer. When the ceremony had been completed, he shook hands with my father. "All over Volhynia," he said, "death, death, death . . . Get out of this area as quickly as you can."

The Ukrainians drove away, and we walked back to our carts, our hearts filled with grief for our murdered people and fear for ourselves.

As we went on, our numbers kept dwindling. It was a joyous reunion when we could all be accounted for, but a week later, when for the third time some of our people did not reach their destination, I looked at Zoya, among the weeping women. She was cuddling her little brother and trying to suppress her sobs.

"Father," I said, "I want to marry Zoya. Before we all perish."

"Don't talk nonsense, son." He gave me a reassuring

126

smile as he collected his thoughts, but his eyes, lit by the camp-fire, remained troubled. "You'll get married. As soon as we reach Hungary."

"And if we don't?"

"Oh, don't be silly." He bent over and slapped my back. "Here, have some food." My mother had just given him some potatoes baked in the fire and he passed a few of them on to me. We dug them from the field in the morning, small, young, light-skinned potatoes which had become our daily staple.

Pawel came over and sat down next to me, and while I shared my food with him, Gregory Mular also joined us. "Mikita is stirring up trouble again," he said.

"He still wants to go back?" Father asked.

"No, this time he says we need a new, more responsible leader. He is shrewd, he doesn't say he should be the one, just anyone but you. You don't know the roads, he says, that's why the people get caught."

"But *I* do," my grandfather interjected, "and I advise my son."

"Don't worry," Mular said. "Nobody listens to Mikita now. They know he is only talking out of anger and hurt pride. They trust you, Dymitr. You have proven to be a good leader. And don't blame yourself for those who have not made it."

Next day we started early. My father did not want to cross the Dniester, because he felt sure that all the bridges would be guarded by the Germans. My grandfather had advised him to turn east where there was a narrow stretch of land between the Dniester and San rivers, and in the afternoon we found ourselves driving over it, out of the Ukraine and into rolling hills. All our people had been told about the route and of the meeting place that night in a birch forest near the village of Latki.

The carts were now moving much slower as the horses pulled uphill over the rough tracks. In front of us white clouds barred the view. Time stretched into long and tedious hours of riding, the clatter of carts and slapping of reins, the monotony of our journey only occasionally relieved by a noisy flock of starlings, bustards plucking the trees, or cranes flying low above our heads. Soon the clouds grew darker and I felt drops of rain on my cheeks and nose. A flash of lightning streaked the sky, followed by rumbling thunder. Suddenly a heavy downpour began. "There!" My father pointed at a wooden area on our right. The carts hurriedly turned into it, leaving me behind to fix a spéra on a roadside tree, to show where we had gone. Completely soaked, I dashed into the wood, where our three carts had already settled under the big trees. I took off my jacket and shirt, and squeezed them out.

It was twilight. We could only hope that, with the darkness falling, those who followed us would either notice the spéra in a bolt of lightning, or just continue for our reunion, a few kilometres away.

The storm lasted an hour, torrential rain hindering our view of the road and obscuring any other sounds. Finally it slackened into a drizzle. My father gave the order to move on. The road turned into sloshing mud, our wheels sinking into it, but our horses, though breathing heavily, plodded on obediently until, at last, we reached the birch forest where we were all supposed to meet.

Two of our groups were already there, apparently having passed by without noticing the spéra or being seen by us. We started to feed the horses, ate some potatoes, this time raw, because we could not start a fire with wet branches; and then, as the other groups arrived, one after another, I went around and counted the carts, the horses and people. No one was missing. We settled into the carts for the night, covering ourselves with our coats.

When I woke up in the morning, the first streaks of daylight were filtering through the trees. The rain had stopped. "It will be a good day for travelling," my father said.

As we drove out of the forest and reached the road, my

father rose in his seat. "Look!" he said excitedly, pointing ahead. We all raised our eyes. There, in front of us, the outlines of mountain tops were just visible in the dawn. "Hungary!" my father said. "There, in those Beskid mountains, lies the border."

The next day, late in the afternoon, we again met some people – thick-bodied Polish highlanders clad in colourful clothes, the men sporting dashing felt hats with feathers, the women in red kerchiefs, tending their sheep in the upland pastures. At the sight of us they raised their eyes, watching us for a long time. My father glanced at us uneasily and finally said, "I suppose there aren't any market-places in this area. They must be wondering who we are and where on earth we can be going."

My grandfather studied the road. It was becoming narrower as the way wound higher and higher into the hills. "We can't ride much further."

My father nodded. "Our carts will not be able to cross the mountain passes. We shall get stuck sooner or later. I only hope we can reach the pine-covered mountainside which we pointed out as our meeting place."

"It doesn't seem very far," Grandfather said. "Maybe, with God's help, we can, but what then?"

"Then we will abandon our carts and ride the horses. Two on a horse – a husband and wife, a brother and sister, sometimes three – a small child behind."

The green pastures gave way to a rocky area, with occasional vegetation jutting up absurdly from the ground. We no longer saw any people. Often our horses could barely squeeze between two boulders on the narrow path where there was not even a trace of wheel ruts, perhaps washed out by the rain, perhaps never existing. I was holding the reins, when suddenly my father's hand clamped over mine. "Stop!" he said. He was looking to his left. About a hundred metres away was a cluster of clay hovels built over mountain caves. There was no sign of life there – no smoke in the

129

chimneys, no carts or horses outside, no dogs roaming around.

"Bergitka Roma," my grandfather said. "The Mountain Gypsies. But they are not nomads, they never travel. Where are they?"

My mother leaned forward from her seat. "There is somebody in there, see?"

A man in tattered clothes was just emerging from behind one of the hovels. He stopped and looked at us. "Wait!" My grandfather jumped to the ground but, as he ran forward, the man started to back away. "We are Gypsies!" my grandfather shouted. "Don't be afraid. Come over here!"

Hesitantly the Mountain Gypsy began to walk towards my grandfather and, after exchanging a few words with him, let himself be brought over to our cart. He was in his sixties, unkempt and unshaven, his felt shoes breaking at the seams. His dark big eyes under bushy brows blinked nervously as he looked at us. "You are Gypsies?" he asked with a tone of disbelief.

"Yes!"

"What Gypsies?"

"Lowland ones, the Polska Roma," my father answered.

"And where do you think you are going?" The man spoke in a dialect different from ours, but easily enough understood because of its mixture of Slovak words, quite similar to Polish ones.

"Hungary," my father said.

"Are you crazy? You can't get across the border." The man wiped his weather-beaten face and narrowed his eyes in painful recollection. "When word reached us that our lives were in danger, we decided to go there because Hungary is so close. Fifty-seven people, all my family, my relatives, my friends, were caught. Some were shot on the spot, some taken away. I managed to feign dead until the Nazis left, then returned here, hoping someone else might too. I have been waiting here for a week. No one has

130

turned up." The Gypsy's voice broke and he suddenly began to sob.

My stomach turned cold. The colour drained from my father's face and he wearily looked at his father and then at me. He summoned all his ebbing courage and managed to say. "We are abandoning our carts and going on horseback. Do you want to come with us?"

The Gypsy looked back at him with blurred eyes. "What for? To be caught again?"

"We shall leave this path and climb through the forest. That way we hope to avoid the frontier guards."

"You are mad! If the Germans don't find you, the German shepherd dogs will. I am not going anywhere. I'd rather wait for my death here, where I have lived all my life, where my parents and their parents are buried." He pointed to the few trees behind the hamlet, which hid a Gypsy cemetery.

"Come with us, please," my grandmother intervened.

"No," the man said firmly. "Go, if you want to, but I won't budge from this place. We shall meet in heaven. If there is a heaven."

It was no use arguing. The man was obdurate. My father picked up the reins, but it took him several slappings before our horse – as if it, too, sensed the danger – started again. As we drove on I glanced back a few times at the Natkins' cart and saw both Zoya and her mother weeping. No one spoke in our cart, neither my grandparents, nor my mother, daring to say anything. Finally I said, "Father, grant me my wish, please. Let me marry Zoya today, so that we may know at least for one night what life is, before that life comes to an end for us."

The sky was fading into shades of violet and blue when we reached the pine forest on the slope of a tall mountain, the tallest in the entire Beskid range of the Carpathians, about ten kilometres from the border. Leaving the spéra and Zoya's little brother, Bolek, on the path to direct those

131

following, we began skirting the mountain. Our carts bumped heavily, but suddenly after about half a kilometre, a small valley clearing with a little stream running through it opened up in front of us, surrounded by a dense towering forest. My father's spirits rose instantly. "This looks like a good safe place to leave our carts." He looked straight at me and managed a smile. "And to marry you, son, if that is what you wish. For one night we shall try to forget the danger and enjoy ourselves. Before we attempt to cross the frontier."

I leaned out of the cart, searching for Zoya. I waved to her. "Tonight!" I shouted. "We are getting married tonight." The girl's drawn face brightened. Her palm touched her lips and she blew me a kiss. Then she turned to her parents to tell them the news. Her mother hugged her, and her father proudly curled his moustache and wagged his finger at me in fun. "I expected it! Nobody can fool Bora Natkin."

"Do we have your permission?" my father asked loudly over his shoulder.

"You have my permission, Shero Rom! And my blessing. Because that is what my daughter wants."

Our carts came to a halt. Presently two more of the groups joined us. The people remained depressed, for word had spread of the fate suffered by the Bergitka Roma and of the peril facing us, but everyone understood that we had no choice but to leave our carts behind, and the forest clearing was probably the best place to do that. And once there, far from the frontier and the path, one could indulge in a little merriment.

The women started collecting berries and mushrooms that had sprung up under the pine trees after the rain. Children who had never properly perceived the danger gladly gathered wild flowers and strewed them over a large flat boulder that was to serve as a table. Fires were started and soup cooked from potato peelings and nettles. "In better times," my grandmother said wistfully, "we would

132

have hunted hedgehogs and squirrels and would have baked maize cakes spiced with cumin and coriander."

Night had fallen. The sky above us was sown with a myriad golden stars, and a bright clear moon illuminated the whole area as though the heavens were aware of the occasion. Suddenly I heard loud voices. One of the last group of carts had just arrived, carrying Mikita and his son among others. They immediately learned about the forthcoming wedding and Mikita started to scream insults at me, at my parents and at the Natkins, invoking his son's engagement and cursing us all for breaking the Gypsy law. But Koro intervened, yelling, "I don't want that slut! Let her rot in hell!" Pawel lurched at Koro and hit him in the chest, but when Mikita picked up a stone and attempted to throw it at Pawel, my uncle Rudolf wrested it from him, and pushed him to the ground. Mikita, gasping, struggled back to his feet. Then, together with his son, swearing Gypsy obscenities under his breath, he disappeared among the trees.

Finally, when the last cart had arrived and a small tent had been set up for me and Zoya, my father ordered the ceremony to begin.

Pawel, my best man, led me, wearing a felt hat borrowed from Bora Natkin, to the Shero Rom. From the other side came Zoya, dressed in white, a garland of flowers on her head, surrounded by bridesmaids. The people of the camp formed a semicircle around us – all but two. Koro and his father were conspicuously absent.

The Shero Rom was waiting for us on the bank of the stream, a handkerchief in his hand. Behind him were gathered the immediate family members of the bride and groom. "Are you, Roman Mirga, taking this girl as your lawful wife of your own free will?" my father asked, looking at me.

"I am," I answered, swallowing hard.

"Are you, Zoya Natkin, taking this man as your lawful husband of your own free will?"

133

"I am," Zoya said firmly.

My father now took our right hands and tied them with the handkerchief. Then he said, "I am throwing the key that locked you two together into the water, so that no one will ever find it, open the lock and separate you." Then he pantomimed the gesture of thrusting an invisible key into the stream. For a moment we all watched the rushing waters as if making sure that the key had disappeared. "I now pronounce you two husband and wife," he said. Grandmother handed him scissors and he cut the handkerchief, completing the wedding ceremony. "T'avel bachtali a terno hai terni!" "Let the young man and the young woman be happy!"

People came forward and shook our hands. From their faces and their forced smiles I could gather that, hard as they tried, they could not shake off their anxiety. Still Pawel, and Zoya's uncles, in accordance with custom, shook small bags of corn over Zoya and me, shouting their best wishes for our health and fertility. Then my grandmother, the Pchuri Daj, picked up a clay jug and broke it over the boulder. Appreciative cries rose as she counted the broken pieces. "Sixty-two," she announced and the crowd broke into applause. For sixty-two years Zoya and I would enjoy a happy life together. The faces around us brightened, for if we were to live that long, the others too would probably survive as well.

My grandfather brought out his bottle of blackberry liqueur and the men in turn took a sip of the drink. The same bottle that only a week ago had served to anoint the dead, was now being used as a toast to life.

My father asked the violinists to play, but they felt in no mood to do so, so he picked up his violin himself, stepped forward and struck up a tune. "Dance!" he ordered in a voice brooking no opposition. And the people, everyone separately, never together, danced to the lilting melody, twirling around, raised hands twisting in the air, their eyes closed as if in a trance – giving themselves to that one wedding dance, oblivious for the moment to their perilous escape, the dwindling numbers of the group and the terror of tomorrow.

Then we began to eat whatever there was to eat – the soup, the mushrooms, and berries for dessert. Someone dug out another bottle. "Drink, drink it all!" my father urged, his cheeks rosy with excitement and alcohol. "Save nothing! There is plenty of Tokay in Hungary!"

Pawel came up and shook my hand, then kissed me on both cheeks. "Congratulations," he said, "from your best man. Can I also be your best friend? For life?"

I glanced at Zoya and her nod only confirmed what I felt. "Yes," I answered solemnly. As my parents and Zoya's parents watched, Pawel and I extended the small fingers of our right hands, hooked them and pronounced in unison. "Mali, mali . . . So tu chasa, manga desa. So me chava, tuke dava . . ." "Friend, friend . . . What you eat, you will share with me. What I eat, I shall share with you."

Our families cheered as we sealed our eternal friendship. "Am I not lucky?" I said, putting my arms around Zoya and Pawel. "A wife and a friend for life. What more could a man ask for?"

"For life itself," my grandmother said wistfully. "That you shall live to enjoy them both."

When the meal was finished, Pawel blindfolded Zoya and me with dark scarves and, hand in hand, sent us to find our tent after spinning us around. The laughter of the children time and again broke the air as they made us trip by crouching in front of us; but finally, almost exhausted, my hand touched the cloth. I pushed Zoya into our wedding tent and followed her. From outside we could hear the voices, wishing me and my bride and my horse a long life. It did not matter, it did not matter at all that I did not own a horse. One day, perhaps in Hungary, I would.

We pulled off our blindfolds. In the light of a kerosene lamp we saw a sheet and a pillow stretched over a few

135

blankets spread on the grass, and a stool on which lay a knotted handkerchief and a doll. Zoya paid no attention to the little bundle filled with sumari, the family heirloom given to the bride by her mother, but, picking up the doll, held it with a beatific smile. It was pricked with needles by her mother against all the evils that Beng, the devil, might have prepared for us.

I raised the pillow where I was expected to find my parents' gift to me. My eyes watered as I took into my hand my father's golden watch and chain. There was a note with it scribbled in Polish. "I promised you a watch, my son, for your birthday on Christmas Day, but we could no longer afford it. Please take my watch. I got it from my father and am now passing it on to you. Keep it for ever and let its time never stop."

Zoya and I looked at each other self-consciously, because neither of us had ever experienced what was now expected of us, to consummate our marriage. But I took her hand and led her to our improvised bed. I lowered her gently and lay next to her, taking her into my arms. My face moved down to hers. As my lips rested on hers, I felt my heart breaking out of its cage. "I love you, Zoya," I whispered; and as I blew out the light, I did not have to say anything else for, in the Gypsy language, 'I love you' and 'I want you' mean the same.

The sun was high when we awoke. No one bothered us, because my father had ordered that we should remain in the forest clearing for the day and travel on our horses that night. As Zoya and I came out and saw all the carts unharnessed and grouped together, Zoya's mother broke away from her family and rushed into the tent. A moment later she reappeared jubilantly with the white sheet spotted with blood, proudly held high above her head, for all to see. I smiled at the old, medieval custom. There would be no pieces of broken clay jug spitefully attached to the tent in the case of the bride turning out not to be a virgin.

136

Zoya had never even kissed Koro. She had married me, not only her body, but her lips untouched by another man.

I went up to my father, who was surrounded by a group of Elders, and kissed him. "Thank you," I said, "for the watch." Then I opened my jacket to show it chained to a buttonhole of my waistcoat.

"Now you are a Rom, my son," my father said. "Only married men are true Gypsies." He patted me on the shoulder, then turned back to the Elders. I could see he was in the middle of an argument. The Elders were insisting that the abandoned carts be burned, in accordance with Gypsy custom. "No," my father answered firmly. "The wind is blowing from the north. The smoke will betray us."

"No one could see it. We are in a valley clearing and the forest around us is dense and tall," Filip Kuchar said.

"Even if the smoke is not seen, the smell of it may give us away. No!" my father said. "How is Szura Greczko?"

"Very ill," Franko Zbar answered. "He has a high fever. He must have caught a bad cold in the rain. The women are taking care of him."

"One of my wife's brothers will carry him on his horse. Make your round, Roman, and count the horses and the people, adults and children separately."

After a while I returned. "Twenty-five horses and fifty-eight people. Fifty adults, five children and three babies."

"Good," my father said. "No one will have to walk."

No man who had two horses protested against lending one to others – not even Mikita, who had reappeared in the camp very docile, too docile for comfort. "I believe," my grandfather said, "he has decided that he had no choice but to stick with us."

All day long my father and I had to go around, to talk people into leaving their possessions behind. They did not want to part with their precious things – and almost all their belongings seemed precious to them. Again my father was adamant. Jewellery might be taken but nothing else, no clothes, no china, no silverware. All that must be left behind, he decreed; any extra load would hamper our journey.

When the sun finally set behind a mountain peak, we were ready to go. All the extra horses had been assigned. While my grandparents would ride together on their own, my father, with Mother and Mara, would ride on a borrowed one, and so would I with Zoya. Her parents would take her little brother with them.

Suddenly we heard a loud flapping of wings. A flock of storks appeared above us. Our eyes turned, following their flight south, the direction we were about to take. "A good omen!" my grandmother cried out. "Bibija, the forest goddess, will protect us!"

The men assembled around my father as he issued his orders. We were to skirt three mountains, all the time travelling in the opposite direction to the polar star. Some three hours later we would reach a highroad which the Gypsies remembered from their past travels across Slovakia to Hungary. When the Germans occupied Czechoslovakia in 1939, they gave part of Slovakia to Hungary and there was now a direct Polish-Hungarian border.

"You don't expect us to ride on the highroad?" Mikita Kowal asked, mockingly.

"Of course not. There is a small village called Kalina on that highroad, remember it?"

"Yes, we do," a number of people answered.

"We used to stop a kilometre away, in a wood with a stream running through it."

"The stream had good trout," Gregory Mular added.

"There," my father continued, "before reaching Kalina, we shall stop for a rest. It is still about two kilometres from the frontier. I will give my final orders then."

Night fell, a good dark night, with just a few stars. Fireflies sparkled about us and crickets began chirping in the bushes of the clearing. I looked around. Everyone was mounting the horses. I helped Zoya, then got up behind

138

her. I felt her body warm against mine. I spurred the animal on. Its hoofs scattered the pebbles and raised clouds of dust among the boulders as my bride and I, and our band of Gypsies, rode on the uneven ground across the Beskid mountains.

9

We laid old Szura Greczko on the ground by the stream. Through the trees in the distance we could see the twinkling lights of Kalina, its people probably enjoying their peaceful suppers unaware that, in the nearby forest, a band of Gypsies was resting after a strenuous uphill ride. The horses, drenched in sweat, were making their way to the water. Little children were crying for food, but we had none, and their mothers were trying to calm them.

"Is he very sick?" my father asked.

My grandmother, squatting by the old man, answered, "His head is on fire." She drew his eyelids open, felt his temples, then took a knotted handkerchief from her bosom. From it she pulled out her rosary beads, a picture of the Black Madonna, and, for added safety, a blackened wax figurine of Beng, the devil. She uttered a litany of prayers and curses, then got up. "I have done all I can for him," she said. "The rest is up to them." She raised her eyes to the clouded sky. "The heavens and hell are fighting for his soul," she whispered.

A few crows were circling over our heads and my grandmother pelted them with the ugliest curses she knew and threw pebbles, but they just flew high, out of her reach. It was a bad omen: but whether for Szura, or for us all, we did not know.

The old man whispered something and I leaned over to hear what he was saying. "Give me my pipe. I want to have my last smoke." I found his long clay pipe and some tobacco in the pocket of his jacket. I filled it and lit it for

140

him. Szura's soft rosy face, with its little sparkling eyes, brightened, darkened, and then lit up again. It happened several times until, suddenly, the rhythm broke. His face remained blurred in darkness. Both his pipe and he were gone.

My father ordered the people to bury him, not in the ground, as we had left our shovels behind, but under a pile of stones and pebbles. It took us half an hour to build a tomb over him. Then, with everyone gathered, my grandfather intoned, "Our Father built an eternal hut, where from now on you will live, Szura. May you rest there in peace." He fashioned a little wooden cross and stuck it among the stones. We all looked up at the sky. There, on its firmament, a star was breaking through a cloud, for when a man dies a new star will light up above him. We saw it and we knew that Szura Greczko had gone to heaven. The angels had won the battle for his soul.

My father looked around, then said, "We shall wait here, perhaps for an hour, perhaps two, until the clouds cover the sky completely. Then we shall start, separately, one family at a time. We shall meet at the Slovak village of Jasna on the other side of the border, in Hungary, where travelling Lowari Gypsies usually camp at this time." He took a deep breath, then added, "We are going on foot."

"What!" Numerous voices rose around me. "What about our horses?"

My father went on: "The safest way is over the mountain top, well away from the frontier posts. The horses cannot possibly make it. And even if they could, they are too easy to spot."

"Never!" Mikita Kowal answered angrily. "I have already lost one horse, and I won't give up my other one." A few of the other men also objected. To them their horses were their family.

"It is my decision as your Shero Rom!" Father insisted.

"You are not *my* Shero Rom!" Mikita snapped back. "Dozens of our people perished under your rule. On

141

horseback we can escape the guards, on foot we cannot."
As a few scattered voices kept up the protest, the former
Shero Rom took two steps towards my father and spoke
furiously to him. "I wanted to pay you back in Hungary for
all you did to me, but I won't have to. The Germans will do
it for me. Go by foot and rot in hell!"

"Why did we leave Brest Litovsk," Filip Kuchar asked,
"if not to save our horses?"

"No," my father answered. "To save our lives."

Mikita, helped by his son, mounted a nearby boulder, so
that everyone could see him. Straightening his heavy-set
figure, he addressed the Gypsies as if he again were their
leader. "You had a good life under my rule. Look what this
bareforytka Roma has brought you! Nothing but misery,
hunger and death! To whom are you going to listen?"

Filip and three other men stepped out of the crowd and
made their way to Mikita's side. All of them, I noticed,
were owners of two horses. Their wives joined them.

"Listen to me!" my father said. "Yes, our brothers
perished, it can't be helped. But you, you survived. Trust
me, just one more time, and you will be safe. I want to see
you tomorrow. Do you understand? I want to see you all
tomorrow. Alive!" But not one of Mikita Kowal's group
moved. My father shook his head, then waved his hand in
resignation.

Mikita and his small band reclaimed their horses and led
them to a spot some fifty metres away from us. They
listened to Mikita's orders, then mounted. We watched
them as they tried at first to climb the mountain, but it rose
so steeply that the horses kept sliding back. My father
started towards them, but before he could reach them,
Mikita, with his son sitting behind him, changed direction
and began skirting the mountain. "Don't do that!" my
father shouted. "Don't go that way! The Germans are more
likely to be in the valleys!" But it was no use. Mikita just
turned in his seat and waved the men to follow him. Father
tried to stop them, catching their bridles and attempting

to talk the men out of their plan, but they spurred their horses on, and my father had to get out of their way or be trampled on. Within a few minutes the band disappeared among the trees and the sound of their animals' hoofs faded away.

The others gathered closer around my father. We were now fifty people out of the original eighty-four that had started out on the journey. Once more Father looked at the sky. The clouds were getting heavier. "Get your horses and tie them to the trees," he said, "and then lie down and rest, before we start climbing."

We were now doing to our horses what we had done a month earlier to our dogs. I went over to Zoya and we lay down on the pine-needled floor of the forest, close to my parents and sister. Zoya clung to me, looking into my eyes for reassurance. I caressed her hair and cheeks. "Try to sleep a little," I said. She closed her eyes, but a moment later opened them and just gazed at me, making me feel ill at ease, because I also was tense and worried. A light wind began to sway the tops of the trees high above us. I shifted about uneasily as I listened to the sound and to the splash of the stream nearby.

Suddenly a distant shot echoed through the mountains, followed by the staccato of machine-guns. I sat up with a start. Zoya grabbed my hand and squeezed it hard. All around people were propping themselves up on their elbows, anxiously. Then, as abruptly as the firing had started, it ceased as if by an order. No further sound of rifle fire came and the people once again lay down.

In the darkness I could just manage to see my watch. It was eleven o'clock. I was tired, too tired to sleep, and there was a restless, gnawing feeling right in the pit of my stomach. Unwanted thoughts kept pushing up into my mind. I tried to fend them off by thinking of my wedding, of my bride of one day lying next to me, of tomorrow and all the days after tomorrow, in a free country, just a few kilometres away.

143

It was about half an hour later when I heard a disquieting noise – the falling of pebbles and the swish of tree branches. Again I raised my head. It was not the wind or a squirrel; someone was making his way towards us. I listened in silence, frightened. And suddenly from the trees emerged a dark figure, at first unrecognisable. But as it staggered towards us, I saw it was Koro. He was alone.

We all rose to our feet. Koro, gasping for air, slumped down on to the ground. "My father is dead!" he cried out. "They are all dead!"

My father grabbed the boy by the shoulders. "What happened? Tell us what happened!"

"The Germans . . ." The boy managed through his frantic efforts to catch his breath. "We ran into a horse patrol before we reached the border. They opened fire and shot everybody . . . I managed to hide. When they left, I saw them, horses and people, all lying on the ground, dead."

A heavy silence fell upon the camp. Finally Gregory Mular said, "They should have listened to their Shero Rom."

"Can I stay with you?" Koro plaintively looked at my father, the fear of possible rejection chiselled in his face.

"Of course you can," my father answered. "You belong to us." He motioned to Tomasz Klimko and his wife. "Take care of the boy," he said. He glanced at the sky, where a few pale stars were still shining despite the encroaching clouds, then he turned to my uncle.

"Rudolf, you will scout the area. Take Pawel with you and send word back by him. If all is clear, we shall follow, one family every five minutes, the young men helping the women, the children and the old." Ruefully he looked around. There were not many old men left. Of the original nine Elders only four remained. "You must all move as quietly as possible, and dart from tree to tree to keep out of sight. Don't go down until you see the lights of the village in the valley, and, hopefully, next to it, of a Gypsy camp."

144

"When do you want us to leave?" Rudolf asked.

"Now. Start right away."

Rudolf waved to his parents, brothers and sisters, then began to ascend the mountain, climbing easily, almost effortlessly, for he was the strongest man in the camp. Pawel followed him, skilfully using the rocks to plant his feet. Occasionally both men glanced over their shoulders, aware of all the eyes riveted upon them before they disappeared in the pine trees that clothed the mountain slope.

Our band dispersed, to make their last-minute preparations. A few of the men walked over to their horses and patted them goodbye. I saw my grandfather talking to his animal and then kissing it on the muzzle. "Are we the first to go?" Mother asked.

"The last," my father answered. "Just as when we crossed the Bug after leaving Brest Litovsk. I must see that everyone gets over the border before us. I don't want anyone saying that my family and I were the first to rush to safety, leaving the others behind."

Half an hour later we saw Pawel sliding noiselessly down the slope. He reached my father. "Rudolf has remained up. A road winds down to the left. We could see two barricades, lit up by hurricane lamps, fifty metres apart, the first guarded by the Germans and the other by the Hungarians."

Father nodded. "The barricades have always been there. In the past they were manned by Polish and Slovak troops."

"You have a good memory, son," my grandfather said.

"I haven't forgotten anything. That road goes through Jasna."

"But on the left," Pawel continued, "quite far down, we could see a lighted shack, with two German sentries guarding it."

"How far down?"

"Oh, at least two hundred metres."

"Good. Any dogs with the soldiers?"

"No."

"All right then," Father said. "We can start now." He motioned to Bora Natkin. "Your family goes first. You will guide them, Pawel." My wife ran into her mother's arms; she hugged Zoya, not letting her go until, finally, her husband pulled his daughter away from his wife, only to draw her to himself in a hard, almost desperate embrace. He pushed her towards her little brother, and Zoya kissed Bolek, who stared at us bewildered, not comprehending all the commotion. "Come on," Bora said curtly to his wife and started up the mountainside. She, holding her boy's hand, and Pawel followed him.

Every few minutes my father ordered a further group to leave. We strained our ears to catch any sound from above, but heard nothing. So far our people had crossed the mountain without incident.

Finally our turn came, shortly after Franko Zbar, his wife and son had left. I took Zoya's hand. Her grip hurt my fingers, but she was looking directly ahead. After a while I had to let her go, for she needed both her hands to help her through the boulders and to hold on to bushes for support. Occasionally I helped her, and my little sister and my grandmother, to get over some difficult place. Bending under the branches, sweating, our mouths dry from effort, we climbed steadily. As we went, the night birds would flutter away or a glistening lizard, awakened from its sleep, would slither off.

We finally reached the mountain top. Back down below, among the trees, I could glimpse moving shadows. They were our horses bunched together and tied to the trees, but unlike our dogs the faithful animals were keeping quiet. No neighing betrayed that they were being left behind, for ever.

In front of us was a large plateau. We rested a while and then went on, heading straight ahead, our footsteps muffled by the pine needles. The air was cold now and the wind blew stronger as we made our way, moving from tree to tree, zigzagging around moss-covered rocks, crossing brooks until, surprisingly, the wooded area ended and another

146

slope, very steep and covered only with bush, appeared before us. My father gestured to all of us to crouch down and crawl. He and I helped the others, and we all finally made it to the top and the shadows of the trees that once again covered the terrain.

I lay behind the trunk of a large tree and looked down into the valley on my right. There I saw the shack, a lamp inside it illuminating a window, and another one over its entrance throwing a wan light on a German soldier pacing up and down, with a bayoneted rifle slung over his shoulder. Then I noticed another soldier coming out of the darkness towards his comrade, and the two began chatting. I turned to my father, a few metres away, and raised two fingers. From where he was he could not see the valley, so he inched towards me to take a look for himself. "Just as Pawel told us," he whispered as if soldiers two hundred metres away could overhear us. He raised his head enough to enable the others to see him, and waved them on, indicating that they keep down as close to the ground as possible.

The area we were moving through kept narrowing until suddenly a view opened up on my left as well. I could see far below the serpentine of an asphalted road, leading to the two barricades, a few hundred metres ahead of us, lit by lamps so that no passing vehicle would crash into them but would halt when flagged down by the soldiers. Zoya was close to me and I motioned to my left with my head. She nodded. "Hungary," she whispered.

I heard a rustling in front of us and then saw some shadows of people rising up and moving forward. I easily recognised the short, pot-bellied figure of Franko Zbar and near him his equally plump wife being helped by her teenage son. But there was another man with them and, as he started again, I saw it was Pawel. The Zbars went on, but Pawel remained, looking back over his shoulder until he spotted me crawling ahead of our group. "What are you doing here?" I asked.

"Rudolf told me to stay behind and to see that everyone got safely across the area. Down in front there is a wide stream which is the border. Most of our people are already on the other side."

Suddenly and unexpectedly I heard the sound of a falling stone tumbling down the mountainside to our right. We all held our breath, but before the stone got caught in a bush, one of the German sentries down below raised his head. For a moment he listened, then I saw him talking to the other guard and pointing up. "Damn, that clumsy wife of Franko!" Pawel cursed under his breath.

A tightness gripped my stomach as I waited and watched, all the others around me glued to the ground in frozen silence. I whispered an inward prayer that the frontier guards would shrug off the noise and resume their pacing, and I hoped that, being that high up, God would hear me more easily. But He didn't. One of the soldiers ran into the shack and then, a moment later, darted out again, leading two German shepherd dogs, passing one of them to his comrade. Then the two men, pulled by their dogs, started up the mountainside, fading into the darkness. "Hurry!" My father's voice reached me. "Hurry as fast as you can!" We all began to rush forward among the trees and boulders blocking our way, hoping to get across the border before the soldiers got to the top.

Abruptly the darkness was pierced by a powerful searchlight from the direction of the shack, its rays revealing that the soldiers were not climbing the slope towards us but making their way fast up to a point ahead of us where the slope was lower and less steep, apparently trying to reach the stream and cut our escape route. The light rose higher, moving back and forth over the mountain top, never catching us as we, mindful of my father's instructions, kept low. We were now engaged in a desperate race. Finally I heard, and a moment later saw the stream, its wild waters lapping against the banks and the huge stones scattered in its bed. Franko, his wife and son were already wading through it.

The rest of us kept close together, except for my grandparents who were falling behind. Suddenly I noticed Pawel turning back to help them. I hesitated, but Zoya was gripping my hand, pulling me forward. We all ran down to the stream and as I reached the bank, I saw, to my great relief, Pawel appearing on the top, dragging my grandmother by the hand, my grandfather close behind them. We dashed into the water, pushing against the torrent.

Then I heard the barking of dogs. I looked over my shoulder again and saw my grandparents plunging into the stream. But Pawel was not with them. The searchlight momentarily revealed soldiers and dogs just emerging from the mountainside, its beam then hitting the tree tops. One of the soldiers turned on a field flashlight and shouted, "Dorthin! Er ist dort! Schnell! Schiess!" A rifle shot reverberated through the mountains. The barking now rose into a howl, as the dogs pulled the soldiers away from us, having apparently lost our scent the moment we entered the water and only sniffing and seeing Pawel running in the opposite direction. Then the Germans disappeared from view.

"Help!" I heard my sister call as she slipped and fell. I pulled her out of the water, and a moment later we all, one after another, reached the other bank of the stream, running quickly into the bushes. I heard another shot and a distant shout. "They got him!" my father cried.

"Why did he leave us?" my grandmother asked, gasping from effort. "He just pushed me forward and ran."

With a lump in my throat I said, "He was trying to divert their attention away from the stream, away from us."

We lay down, well covered now by the bushes, not daring to move, listening to the snatches of German voices and the vicious barking of the dogs, and watching the searchlight still scanning the area. Then the Germans and their animals appeared once more on the top of the mountain. "Beleuchte den Bach!" I heard. The beam of a field flashlight now hit the stream, moved over it and the bushes hiding us, and then it went off.

149

"Nichts! Er war allein!" the other man answered.

The German voices faded away and the dogs stopped barking. From where I was I could see the two soldiers and their dogs descending again towards the shack. Then the light snapped off and the whole area was thrown into darkness.

My father lifted his head. "Look there!" Excitedly, he was pointing to the gleaming lights of a village in the valley below us. "Jasna," he said. "We made it! We are in Hungary." He embraced my mother, and my sister crawled to them and burst into grateful tears. Suddenly I found myself jumping to my feet and running towards the stream. "What are you doing? Come back!" my father cried after me.

"I must find Pawel! He may be alive. Wounded but alive."

"It's no use! Come back, do you hear me?!"

I started to wade across the stream as if drawn by an irresistible force. It was the first time in my life that I had disobeyed my father. The voices of my parents, my wife and my sister kept ringing in my ears, as I reached the other side and then climbed up the hill to where I felt the Kelderari boy, to whom I had pledged eternal friendship, must be lying.

I groped through the forest, seeing almost nothing, guided by the gleam of a single star that remained in the sky. Then I heard a groan and followed the sound until I reached a shrouded figure on the ground. "Pawel!" I whispered and bent down. "I have come for you."

From the boy's drawn lips came a moan and his hand clasped at his chest. I unbuttoned his torn jacket; beneath it his shirt was soaked in blood. I tore off the cloth. The bullet had penetrated the hollow of his throat. "The Germans?" I finally made out what he was saying.

"They have gone," I answered, trying to lift him.

"And your family?"

"They are all safe on the other side."

He nodded with satisfaction. "It is good to have a family." Then he began to cough blood, and I realised that the soldiers had left him to bleed to death.

There was no use trying to help him. All I could do was stay with him. Then his hand slid from his chest to the ground. "Pawel!" I cried out. Gently, I touched the little square cloth bag suspended from his neck, the bajero which all Kelderari parents hang on their baby boys, with a seed and a piece of iron inside, to assure their health and strength in life.

Swallowing the tears that welled into my throat I said, "Goodbye, my friend." Then with a heavy heart I rose and went back, through the forest, down the slope across the stream, to where my family was waiting. They asked no questions. "Come," my father said, putting his arm around me.

We started towards the village, Zoya holding my hand. After a while we came out of the trees and bushes. The lit-up barricades on our left were far behind us. My grandfather raised his head. "Those other lights, to the right of the village," he said, "that's the Lowari camp. Our people are probably there already, waiting for their Shero Rom."

The mist, drifting and low, was starting to rise and chase the darkness away. The sky began to grow pale as we walked, soaking wet but safe and unafraid, into the dawn of a new day.

10

Fires were burning all over the camp, the wood pleasantly crackling. Aromas of lard, ham, and sausages cooked with whole cabbage leaves, permeated the entire area, while the musicians were tuning up their instruments and the dancers limbering up. The Lowari were preparing a feast in honour of their guests. We were heroes. We had defied the most powerful gadje military might in the world, triumphed over hunger and exhaustion and, when deprived of our carts, had travelled bareback on our horses, and when deprived of our horses, had walked, crossing the thickly forested mountains and the heavily guarded frontier to reach freedom. We were true descendants of Pharaoh's brave Gypsies who had once ruled the world, and the camp bards were already composing odes to our epic feat, to be sung, and passed on from father to son and mother to daughter, for generations to come.

Earlier that day our Gypsies, who had crossed the border before my family, had assembled outside the encampment, waiting for their Shero Rom. It was only after seeing my father safe and sound, and when everyone had had a chance to embrace him and thank him for saving their lives, that they were ready to be led by him into the camp. The children who saw us began to edge away and run back to their mothers as the women came out of their wagons to discover the cause of the commotion. The women called their men and they all watched us approach with apprehension, while a pack of dogs rushed howling towards us. We then became aware that we must look like gadje in our clothes purchased from Ukrainian peasants, the men wearing peaked caps over trimmed hair, the women colourful babushkas tied under their chins. My grandfather, Sandu, burst out laughing. "Na daran, Romale, wi ame sam Romaczacze!" he shouted. "Don't be afraid, Gypsies. We are Gypsies too!"

They understood and immediately surged towards us. Their Slovak Gypsy dialect was similar to ours, they plied us with questions, and then led us all, the entire band of fifty, past old men sitting with their clay pipes on upturned buckets and old women weaving baskets, and past the big corral containing many horses, until we reached the biggest and most beautifully oranamented wagon in the camp. "Janko Zadar!" they called, and out stepped a robust Lowari chieftain, proud of his huge walrus moustache and set of gold teeth, wearing wide pantaloons tucked into long boots and a silver-buttoned waistcoat with a watch-chain of gold coins. He looked all of us over, not understanding, but hearing from all sides the exclamations that we, too, were Gypsies, he stretched out his hand to my father.

"Same Romandyr san? And from what Gypsy tribe are you?"

"Polska Roma," my father answered, and then explained our disguise. "We have escaped from Poland, from the Germans."

The man opened his mouth in amazement, looked towards the Beskid mountains, then threw his arms around my father and eagerly asked for details. "They tried before," he said. "Others. But none of them made it. It's hell there, isn't it? Hell and death."

My father told him about the warning we received in Brest Litovsk from a Polish nobleman, the ghetto emptied of the Kelderari, the Sobibor concentration camp, the mass execution of the Lowari on the road to Lukov, and the loss of many of our own people before the rest had finally made it in carts, then on horseback, then on foot. We heard cries of pity and sorrow all around us, and then Janko clapped his hands. "Open your wagons to our guests," he ordered. "Feed them, pour water for those who want to wash and shave, and let them sleep and sleep all day. In the evening we shall have a feast."

A swarthy young couple, married a few months earlier, took in Zoya and me, let us wash and eat, asking no questions, for we were dropping from fatigue. They pointed to their own bedding spread on straw mattresses on the floor. We lay down and immediately fell into a deep sleep.

When I awoke, it was dark. We had slept twelve hours. We were alone in the wagon. A small paraffin lamp hung on the wall among holy pictures and in its light I could see my bride, rested and beautiful, her unblinking eyes watching me with a glint of pride, her lovely mouth curled in a smile. "My husband!" She repeated the word time and again, and then cuddled into my arms. Only now had the full impact of her being married to me reached her. She kissed me on the shoulder, my cheek, my hand. "It's all over," she whispered. "The nightmare."

The scents of food, the crackling fires, and the sound of music brought us to our feet. Our hosts were waiting for us outside, sitting on stools, already dressed in their best clothes. The young man took mine and the young woman Zoya's hand, and led us to the centre of their encampment. It was already filled by their colourfully attired women – glistening stones knotted into their braids, strings of coins around their necks – forming one group, and their men, dressed in waistcoats, wide pantaloons, long boots and felt hats, gathered on the other side. I was ushered to a place right behind two armchairs on which sat the two Shero Roms – Janko and my father. Next to me was my grandfather and three other surviving Elders of our kumpania – Franko Zbar, Gregory Mular and Tomasz Klimko. Zoya joined the women. The men all drank and soon I too was served barack pálinka, the potent colourless apricot brandy. This time I did not dislike the drink. I was a married Rom, a man. Both the Lowari chieftain and my

154

father were, literally, in high spirits. "Mountain will not get together with mountain. Never!" my father was saying, his arm around Janko Zadar, "But man with man, yes!"

The fiery-looking Slovak Gypsy twirled the edges of his moustache. "We have a saying, Dymitr" – the two Shero Roms were already on first-name terms – "I with my brother against my cousin. I with my cousin against the gadje." And he, in turn, threw his huge arm around my father's shoulder and called for more pálinka.

We gorged ourselves on the food, and gulped a delicious borscht made from wild cherries and meat, and seasoned with sour ant juice. We devoured stuffed cabbage that reminded me of the beloved Polish bigos which my grandmother used to make for us. And finally we had delicious palacsintas, thin pancakes with raspberry jam, topped with mounds of real cream, the like of which I had not seen since Warsaw.

My grandfather and the other Elders now joined the old Lowari men and smoked their strong black Hungarian cigarettes. Among the women I could see Zoya, my mother and hers, and my aunt Irina who was eating while breast-feeding her baby. Every one of our people looked happy, intoxicated with food, alcohol and freedom.

Our host clapped his hands, raised his silver cane and the concert began. We watched the dances, the Slav kolo and the Hungarian csárdas, and then enjoyed the fiddlers playing their lilting melodies. Finally we listened to the ballads composed in our honour. What a beautiful evening it was. My father's face was flushed with excitement and his dimple stood out more vividly than usual, as time and again he brushed his moustache, proud of having led so many of his people to safety. Then he turned and patted me on my knee, as he used to do before I got married, when I was still a boy. "Isn't it wonderful to be a Gypsy?" he asked.

"How far is Budapest?" I asked soberly.

155

"Budapest?" My father's eyes blinked. "Who is going to Budapest?"

"Aren't we?" I asked. "To work there, like we did in Warsaw."

Janko Zadar heard us and he turned to me. "There are a hundred Gypsy orchestras in Budapest," he said. "The Hungarian Gypsies don't even talk or sing Romany, only that horrible Hungarian. You'll break your tongue on it. We've been here for four years since this province became Hungarian, but we have not even tried to learn the language."

My father raised his forefinger, both to me and the Lowari chieftain. "I am the Shero Rom," he said, "and I will not leave my kumpania."

"Of course not," Janko Zadar said. "We have our duty towards our people."

I was taken aback. When my father had spoken of Hungary, I had seen in my mind's eye Budapest. When he spoke of freedom, I saw a nice job in a night club for all of us, including Zoya, and a good apartment, and a school for Mara – not for me, I was too old, but for Mara. "What shall we do then?" I asked.

"Travel," my father answered.

"Right! Drom Romano, the Gypsy road," Janko said. "The Gypsy forest, the Gypsy river . . . But forget the south, don't mix with the Hungarians, stay here as we do, travel along the Slovak border, all the way to Austria and back. The peasants there are Slovaks, or they understand Slovak. Your women can tell fortunes, your men can do ironwork, your musicians and dancers can perform. But if you go into the rest of Hungary, you'll starve. Is this a bad life we have? Look around."

"No," my father said. "It's a great life."

Later that evening when our band had gathered together the people, remembering that we had lived in Warsaw, anxiously asked my father about his plans. He raised both his hands. "Don't worry, I'm not planning to leave you.

156

Never again." The men slapped each other's backs in relief and jubilation. I knew that my father, and perhaps even my mother, were like wild animals who had been caught and tamed and had performed for big-city people; but once released back into the jungle, they eagerly took to their old way of life.

Exhausted, filled with food and drink, we returned to our wagons, knowing we would have to squeeze in with our hosts for the night's rest. I then noticed Koro Kowal. He had not joined in the celebration. He was alone, clad in a black shirt, sitting by a fire he had built himself, a few candles burning in front of him, only now able to mourn his father in the Gypsy way. He could not participate in the general merriment and would keep away from it for a whole year. He did not drink the pálinka offered him, but flicked drops of it on to the ground as a benediction for his father's soul. Then, with a jug in his hand, he splashed fistfuls of water around the fire to quench his father's thirst, while the candles he had lit were to light the way and the fire to keep Mikita Kowal warm on his voyage to heaven.

Zoya took my hand and we walked, unnoticed by Koro, into our wagon, but as I lay on the floor, beside my wife, squeezed between our Lowari hosts, I could not help thinking that the alcohol and water sprinkled over the ground, and the candles and fire, were also in memory of the thirty-four people of our kumpania who had never made it to the promised land.

Again I slept soundly like a beaver. When I woke up next morning and got up, before Zoya, I was treated by my host to real coffee cooked in a pot on an open fire. Then I went in search of my father and found him with Janko outside his wagon, sitting in armchairs and sipping hot tea through lumps of sugar held in their mouths. They offered me a glass and I took it. Tea was always good after coffee, it washed it down. When Janko finished his drink, he rubbed

157

his big hands and then pushed his felt hat back with the tip of his thumb.

"Well," he said to my father. "Celebrations over, let's get down to business." I could see him unveil his gold teeth in an anticipating smile.

"What business?" my father asked.

"Horses," the man said. "The Lowari are horse-traders. And you don't have horses."

"Of course," my father said. "But what about the wagons?"

"We also have wagons. At least ten spare wagons for sale. And also some of the other things you need. Gypsy clothing for the men and women, pots, dishes and cutlery, buckets, basins . . . You have nothing, you have to start your life again."

"That's right, we have nothing," my father sighed. "No money either."

Janko grinned. "But you have jewellery. Sewn into your clothing, right?"

"Yes, jewellery we have."

The man rubbed his hands again. "We accept jewellery," he said, "and will give you a good price."

The two men discussed the deal for the next hour. Then I was sent to collect the jewellery from the others and to note everything I was given down on paper, who gave what, so that the private property of gold and precious stones would be converted into the private ownership of horses and wagons. The Lowari and our Elders joined the discussion, and finally all the men took part in the bargaining. This, interspersed with eating and drinking, lasted a long time, but before the day was over, the business had been concluded and we found ourselves the proud owners of almost everything we needed in order to resume the normal nomadic life of a Gypsy tribe.

When we finally retired for our last night in the camp, my father said, "They got the better of the bargain. The Lowari are shrewd. Good people, warm-hearted, but

158

shrewd. Well," he added with a wry smile, "it can't be helped. After all we are not their brothers, only their cousins."

What a wonderful summer that was! Very soon I stopped thinking of Budapest and took to the Gypsy ways like a duck to water, like a young cub being returned to the jungle. I could hardly remember the spring-summer-and-autumn wanderings of my childhood. And our escape to Hungary from Poland was too terror-filled to give me the true flavour of that way of life. But my young wife also adored it and enthused me with her passion for freedom and for nature, its landscapes continuously changing in front of us, as our wagons drove on slowly enough for our eyes to have time to feast on the expanse of the blue sky and the green meadows, the multi-coloured chequerboard fields of wheat, oats and potatoes and the swaying walls of corn and sunflowers. "Look, look!" Zoya would shout in joy, eager to share with me the delight of following a flight of swallows above our heads or swarms of butterflies fluttering among the field flowers, to listen to the sounds of streams rushing between banks or the plopping of fish in a pool.

Oh, how I learned to love the noise of rattling wheels and creaking axles, the crack of a whip, the soughing of the wind, the rustling of a tree, and the hum of flies and bees accompanying us on our journey. My father was right, and before him my grandfather and my great-grandfather. Like storks, flying from nest to nest, we moved from forest to forest, wesz weszestyr, tanned to deep brown by the summer sun, smearing ourselves with walnut oil to look even darker and more manly, always driven by a longing for the unknown, then halting at dusk for the night, or sometimes a few nights. And then, when fires had been struck all over the encampment and scents of burning wood, roasted acorns and coriander and rosemary filled the air, the black iron kettles would sing over the trivets, or the plaintive melody of a violin would float across the camp, Zoya and I would clasp our hands, our hearts beating in the same blissful rhythm. Sleeping on the soft grass, we gained a sense of rest and peace from the timelessness of the moment, the star-studded sky, the song of a nightingale, the cry of babies and the barking of dogs from a distant Slovak village. And what lovelier awaking could there be than opening one's eyes to the call of a lark, the rustle of leaves above us, the neighing of hungry horses and the rap of our ironsmiths' hammers, already at work.

With the remaining jewellery and gold our men bought themselves tools, anvils and bellows, and our musicians new instruments. But our best times were when we came to the fairs or amusement parks. There our women, under the direction of my grandmother Rosa, would set up the ofisurias in booths or tents, decorate them with bibles, statues of saints, pictures of the Black Madonna and black figurines of Beng the devil, and tell fortunes from cards, hands or coffee grounds. Our musicians, dancers or wrestlers would perform, and our family group, now joined by both Zoya and Mara dancing, did particularly well, with my little sister's hat filled with florints, especially after my father had been playing his violin. Soon we bought another wagon, so now Zoya and I had our own, its wheels hooped with brass and copper ornaments, its windows covered by lace curtains, silver-framed holy and family pictures as well as twigs of artificial flowers adorning its walls.

We travelled, as the Lowari chieftain had advised us, all the way along the Slovak border, from the Beskid to the Pilis mountains, from the Tisha to the Danube rivers, from Jasna and Tokay to Gyor near where the Czech and Austrian borders met the Slovak one. Sometimes we encountered hostility, especially among the Hungarian peasants. But they rarely closed their homes to us, or shouted "Szigany, move on!", although after making a trade with us they would often throw chips of burning coal after us or spit three times on the ground. This did not bother us: the fear of a Gypsy curse, of our evil eye, dies hard. It was part of our life, part of being a Gypsy.

The summer turned into autumn. The wind began blowing from the east as our caravan was making its way through ancient small towns with their cobblestone lanes and the villages with white huts on both sides of their main, and only, street. Still the trees provided us with fruit, the vine with sweet grapes, the streams with fish, the forest with game. But we no longer slept on the ground, we moved into our wagons.

We found a place on the bank of the Danube near Rajka, well protected from storms and among friendly villagers who promised to order chains, scythes and sickles from us and to employ our musicians and dancers for the St Nicholas, Christmas and Three Kings' feast days. The winter finally came, but this was as it should be. God created the seasons. Still, we Gypsies prefer one summer to seven winters. That summer, the most memorable and lovely summer of my life, was worth seven winters. That year in Hungary had been worth seven years of our lives.

PART TWO

1

Spring came early that year and warmed our camp, as it speckled the meadows with poppies, buttercups and corn-flowers, and clothed the trees with fresh foliage. The winding roads shaded by poplars and silver birches irresistibly lured us to move on. There were no more holidays on the Christian calendar; the fiddlers and dancers grew restless; our ironsmiths had done all the work ordered from them by the villagers and now they sat idly, smoking and swapping tales of bygone days. Only the women, accustomed to support their men when the men did not work, could bring the florints home, their babies strapped to their waists by wide shawls and sucking their mothers' breasts while the mothers told fortunes to gullible and hopeful peasants. So one day my father called the Council of Elders, to which new men had been added to make it nine strong, since nine it had to be because of long tradition and the good luck attached to that number. They unanimously decided it was time to resume travelling, and made plans to cross the steppes of the Hungarian prairies towards the Matra mountains.

It took us a day to pack. We started at dawn, making our way out of the forest clearing over a rutted path until we reached the road leading south from Rajka. We hoped to get to Mosonmagyaróvár by ten o'clock, to take part in the fair that was part of that town's spring cattle market. We had the road to ourselves, except for an occasional horse-cart, unhurriedly driven by a half-sleepy man. My father, as usual, drove first and I was right behind him in our twelve-wagon caravan. The dogs, tethered to the axles, ran alongside. The morning dew shone on the grass and the fields shimmered in the light of the rising sun. "It's going to be a lovely day," Zoya said, smiling at the sight of blossoming fruit shrubs. Thick-bodied peasants were already in the fields, preparing the ground for seeding their crops, repairing their wooden fences or scarecrows torn down by winds. From the barns with their tattered roofs came the familiar smell of stored hay and fresh manure. Through open gates we saw kerchiefed women sitting on low stools, milking their cows. My father turned to look over his shoulder and waved at me. Zoya reached for a small pot resting at her feet, untied the cloth covering it and offered me bread dipped in chicken fat, to be washed down by sweetened tea from a kettle.

It was around eight when our road joined the highway running from the Austrian border. There were now more carts and even some motor-cars passing us. There was also a distant roar and I saw some planes, so high in the sky that they were only glittering silver specks gliding to the east.

We travelled on past white-walled villages and hills where barefoot shepherd boys with their dogs were driving flocks of sheep, past decayed chapels centuries-old or gilded figures of Christ nailed to a wooden cross. Again I heard a heavy rumble, but this time far on the road behind us, slowly and unmistakably coming nearer. I looked back, but we were on the bend of the highway and I could not see anything. The noise now grew louder. Suddenly there were three tanks lumbering forward, straddling the entire road, soldiers' heads sticking out of the turrets. The tanks were followed by an endless line of open trucks in which, in rows five abreast, sat helmeted soldiers with rifles and fixed bayonets. Their uniforms were grey-green and they were Germans.

"Oh, God!" Zoya whispered, her face turning pale. My stomach turned cold and my whole body went limp.

Blocked by our caravan, the motorised column halted.

166

Our Gypsies yelled at their horses and pulled their reins hard to the side in a frantic effort to get out of the way, but there was a wide ditch running alongside the road. I heard angry German voices and then saw a half-track coming fast from behind and halting at the front wagon. A German lieutenant leaned out of it. "Hey, Sinti!" he shouted to my father. "You're in our way. Get out of here!"

My father spurred his horse on and we all followed, trying as quickly as possible to reach some unseen point ahead where the ditches on both sides of the road would end and give us a chance of turning aside. Suddenly a black Mercedes swept past and screeched to a stop. A tall colonel, wearing a monocle, jumped out, followed by his aide. "Halt!" he bellowed. "Where do you think you're going?"

"We can't turn here," my father answered in German, pulling in his reins.

"Ausweis!" the man snapped.

I saw my father digging nervously into his clothes and, after a frenzied search, pulling out his documents. Drops of sweat showed on his forehead as he handed the papers over to the officer.

"Polnishe Sinti?" The colonel turned to his aide. "Warum sind die auf dem Weg, nicht in Auschwitz?" Then he ordered "Push all the wagons into the ditch! They are in our way."

The young captain saluted and jumped on to the half-track, motioning its driver to back past our wagons and the tanks. "Please, sir, have mercy!" my father implored the colonel, while my grandmother ran to him, carrying the picture of the Black Madonna and shouting, "We are Christians!" in Gypsy, then Polish. The man callously pushed her aside, then wiped his hand against his uniform as if she were a leper.

From all of the wagons our people anxiously hurried towards us. Then soldiers ran forward, slinging their rifles across their shoulders as they did so, a few of them stopping at each of the wagons. Methodically, together and with yells of "Zusammen! Jetzt! Nur ein Mal!", they began pushing the wagons into the wide ditch, unmoved by the horrified cries of their owners, the hysterical sobbing of children and the tearful implorings of women, stooping to kiss their boots. Some of the Gypsies barely managed to jump down before their wagons were pushed over. From my drawn lips came a cry of pain and fright. Near me, Zoya, her eyes brimming with tears, her body shaken by a half-smothered cry, looked at me time and again as if I could do something to stop the Germans. One after another, with a resounding crash, the wagons were capsized into the ditch, as the horses harnessed to them, whinnying wildly and rearing on their hind legs in terror, were forced over on to their rumps. The dogs howled in panic, but some succeeded in tearing themselves loose and hurled themselves at the soldiers. Shots rang out as the men coldly gunned them down, pumping several bullets into each of the attacking animals, tearing their bodies to shreds.

"I'm sorry for the horses," the colonel said. "Shoot them!"

A hollow wail arose from the Gypsies around me. I watched helplessly, glued to the spot with impotent rage as, one after another, our horses and the remaining dogs were shot. Nearby my sister Mara hid herself in the folds of my mother's skirt, her little body trembling, trying to find solace by turning her back to and her eyes away from the horror of the Nazis and their rifles. Unbelievingly, I saw my father's violin in my mother's hand. Apparently she had grabbed it when jumping down from their wagon, holding Mara with one hand, and my father's instrument with the other.

The colonel's aide returned on the half-track. He stepped down. "What about the people?" he asked his commanding officer, pointing to the Gypsies huddling together in terror behind my father.

"Get them into the half-empty trucks at the back of the

column. Drive them across the border and hand them over to the commander of the nearest railway station. He will send them where they belong."

Brisk orders were issued and the soldiers immediately rounded up our people. My legs felt heavy and my lungs ached. I held Zoya's hand as, with my parents with Mara and my grandparents right behind me, and the rest gathered in family groups, we were marched past our slaughtered horses and dogs and overturned wagons, past the roaring tanks, mockingly swinging their turrets at us, and past the truckloads of soldiers anxious to move on to further conquests.

We reached the open trucks, loaded half with shells and half with cartons of canned food. The soldiers forced us all – men and women and even the children – at gunpoint to transfer the cargo to other trucks. Unexpectedly Jan Michalak lurched towards a portly corporal holding a machine-gun, but before he could reach him, the man jammed his barrel into the Gypsy's stomach. Jan doubled up in pain. "Next time I'll shoot you like a dog!" the German snarled and booted him into line.

"Up, into the trucks," the captain ordered. Meekly the Gypsies clambered into the vehicles. We were loaded like sacks of potatoes, thrown together with hardly space to breathe, twenty-five to each truck. I could hear the noise of the motorised column now resuming its way towards Budapest. Our vehicles turned around on the highway and, followed by the half-track with a machine-gun trained on us, drove back the way we had come, but then after a few minutes turned towards the Austrian border.

My whole body ached as if it had been beaten by rods. Close to me I saw Zoya's wilted mouth, Mara still shaken by small, sweeping sobs, my mother's face contorted in agony, my grandmother Rosa wringing her hands and moaning. All around me men were paralysed with fear, old women muttered curses and the children, clinging to their mothers' bodies, cried desperately.

169

"Where are they taking us?" Zoya whispered, her face paper-white.

"I don't know."

"What's Auschwitz?"

"I don't know."

Suddenly I saw my father mopping the sweat from his face. He reached for his violin in my mother's hand and managed to swing it under his chin. In that terrible hour of anguish he started to play Liszt's famous Hungarian Rhapsody. The adults fell silent, the children stopped weeping, all of them startled and yet calmed by the music. Some of the people even managed brave smiles. And my father, his face again haggard, went on playing Gypsy tunes in this, perhaps single, act of defiance of the Nazis who – on that beautiful day of March 19, 1944, which never had a chance to blossom into spring for us – invaded Hungary.

We were driven at a snail's pace on a highway clogged with tanks, trucks, marching soldiers and motor-cyclists whose machine-guns were mounted on their handlebars. A smell of cordite, diesel fuel and exhaust fumes filled the air. Along the road peasants had stopped working in the fields and stood, shovels in their hands, gaping at the armed intruders. I saw a raised iron barrier and realised that, only a few hours before, this had been a frontier. The Hungarian border guards had been disarmed and herded into the Customs building where they were staring out of the windows in stoical silence, as column after column of German soldiers drove by. We passed another barrier, the Austrian side of the border, and here the guards were on duty as if this were a normal day of international traffic. A kilometre or so beyond the frontier, there were German flags on tall poles at the roadside, fluttering in the light wind, interspersed with huge portraits of Hitler. Then villages appeared, with German names and signboards over empty shop windows.

As we drove through the streets, everyone stared at us,

170

the only vehicles going in the opposite direction, but no-body waved. We entered the old town of Nickelsdorf and halted in front of the station building which was guarded by a detachment of soldiers. Our guards rushed to get us down fast with the help of their rifle butts, while the captain signalled at the station for assistance. They joined their colleagues with raucous laughter and jokes about the first prisoners-of-war being taken in the armed assault on Hungary. A German staff officer, passing by in his car, jumped out, focused his camera on us, took a picture, and then drove off again.

A chubby major rushed out of the station building. The young captain raised his hand in the Nazi salute and the major responded. Then the captain reported that we were a band of Gypsies they had encountered on the road and that it was his duty to put us on the first freight train to Auschwitz. "Obersturmbannführer Eichmann," he added, "is already in Budapest and that's what we are sure he would wish us to do." Once again Zoya looked at me questioningly, but I was still unable to answer her. Never before had I heard the name 'Auschwitz', nor had I any idea what or where it was. The officers lowered their voices and I could hear nothing more, then I saw the guards who had brought us climb back on to the half-track and drive away, leaving us in the hands of the paunchy major.

The icy feeling in the pit of my stomach lingered as we were led through the station hall on to the platform filled with platoons of soldiers boarding a passenger train. Guarded on all sides by the soldiers, who kept their rifles trained on us, we walked across railway lines, past shunting wagons and whistling locomotives, through steam and smoke, until we reached the end of the station yard. We were then marched past a red signal, to an empty wagon. It was not a freight truck, but a cattle truck. The soldiers slid open its heavy doors, threw down a wooden ramp, and the major commanded, "Get inside!" He smiled at the sight of the violin in my father's hand, but did not take it away from

171

him. When all fifty of us had filled the wagon, the door was slammed back into place behind us. As the bars were bolted and the voices of the soldiers receded, our women and children again burst into a wailing chorus. The wagon was dark, except for streaks of light from two animal ventilation slats. I tried to summon a little courage to cheer Zoya, just as my father attempted to calm his family down. But to no avail. The faces around me, half-shadowed, spoke of terror. We were trapped, and filled with the foreboding that Auschwitz might be another Sobibor.

We were huddled together like cattle, standing, because there was just room enough for the old people to sit on the floor. We exchanged places at the ventilation slats frequently in order to share a whiff of fresh air and a glimpse of the outside world. That view was a sentry with his rifle marching up and down the length of our truck. From the distance came the eternal railway noises – the clash of wagons and the shunting of engines, relieved on the hour by the faraway chimes of a town clock. It was afternoon when a new guard replaced the old one and he carried a sack with him. Out of it he dug some loaves of black bread and threw them, one by one, into our wagon through one of the slats. "Water, please!" Zela Mular called. The man shrugged. My aunt Irina lifted her one-year-old Puji to show the man, shouting, "Wasser! Wasser für mein Kind!" The man spread out his hands as if to explain that he was doing what he was ordered and could do no more. Somebody up there, perhaps the major, had remembered that we had to eat; somehow it had not occurred to him that, even if we were cattle, we still had to drink.

My uncle Rudolf sized up the new guard. He was an older man with a moustache, probably an Austrian peasant drafted into non-combat duty. Rudolf summoned a few young men and together they tried to pull the door from inside, irrationally hoping that they could prise it open and then perhaps overwhelm the man. But the iron bars held;

172

they did not even make a sound. My uncle gave up. Then my brave little wife started a song, the song that my mother always sang: "From village to village Gypsy girls are strolling . . ."

A few other girls pushed themselves to the truck's door and picked up the tune, "They are strolling and telling fortunes . . ." They sang to the guard and smiled at him. The man looked surprised, came closer to the wagon and listened with a grin on his face. He enjoyed the tune, and when the women had finished, he clapped his hands and asked for more "Wasser, bitte!" my aunt Irina said again, once more lifting Puji into view. The man looked around uncomfortably, then discovered a tap some thirty yards away and looked around for a can or bottle. My father threw out his felt hat. The man nodded, went to the tap and filled it with water, and then carried it back to us. We passed round the hat, drinking from it one after another, and the guard obligingly refilled it. The girls broke into another song. The Gypsy singing was paying off.

The afternoon passed into evening, the evening into night. The moon, particularly bright and clear, shone through the ventilation slats. The old guard was replaced by a new, younger one who brought no food and no water. We talked very little as most of our people, even those standing, were dozing. Only my father and a few of the young men kept watch. They gazed unblinkingly into the distance and avoided looking directly at each other, so that no questions would be asked, questions that could only cause pain and provide no answers. Then, in the middle of the night, from out of the station's continuous rumble came the chug-chug of a locomotive. I stuck my head out and could see it coming from behind on our line. We felt a jolt. Railwaymen jumped down and attached our wagon to it. We were pulled back into the station, then changed rails and pushed forward on another track. "What's happening?" people asked anxiously and my father, looking out of the other slat, told them what we saw. I thought we were going to crash into a row of wagons, as the locomotive pushed us towards them, but then it slowed down. Again railwaymen jumped down and attached us to a waiting train. This time they disengaged us from the engine, which pulled away.

Only now did I realise that the platform was full of armed soldiers, directed by the same fat major in whose charge we had been left. The train consisted of five cattle trucks, preceded by another locomotive already puffing and whistling as if raring to go. I managed to lean out further and then saw that the doors of all the wagons of the train were bolted and barred and that chalked on the wagons were signs with huge Stars of David and the word 'Juden'. I caught sight of bearded faces looking out of their ventilation slats. Our Gypsy truck had been attached to a Jewish transport and we were going to wherever those Jews were going.

With an anguished shriek of its engine, as if it were crying for us, the train pulled out, with soldiers settling on the running boards between the trucks, rifles in their hands, and the major waving goodbye to his men, smiling with satisfaction at a well-fulfilled assignment. The clacking wheels picked up speed as we changed rails, passed by a green signal, and left the station and the drab buildings of Nickelsdorf behind us. With a lump in my throat, but trying to keep my voice steady, I relayed to those behind me what was happening. Once more the lament of the women and children filled the car. Zoya clung closer to me. Other women cradled their arms around their children and propped themselves against their husbands both for consolation and to support their swaying bodies. Mara started to cry and again pressed her head against my mother's bosom. "I left Mirka in the wagon," she whimpered with anguish. My little sister cried not for herself and us; she wept for her doll, abandoned and probably crushed in a ditch in the Hungarian countryside.

For a while we ran past dimly lit stations that loomed up from time to time, and then I noticed that the stations' names had changed. They now had signs similar to Polish ones, yet they were not Polish. My father looked out and said, "We are passing through Czechoslovakia."

The train rode quietly through the night. The sky was filled with stars and, as I watched the Gypsy Carriage, the Great Bear constellation, I could not help recalling happier times when Zoya and I had ridden in Count Paszkowski's sleigh on New Year's Eve. Sleeping Moravian cities, with pale streets winding narrowly away, barely lit by sickly yellow lamps, or white-walled villages with red-tiled roofs, were passing by us. There were no civilians out of doors, and house shutters were closed against the war, while the Germans and the cattle trains carried people to concentration camps.

Dawn slowly began to break and violet lights descended on to the chequered fields and the small towns dominated by the steeples of Catholic churches. It was already daylight when we stopped for a few minutes at a station named 'Těšin'. Ten minutes later we slowed down again, and as I looked out at the station building, I saw the name 'Cieszyn' on it. We were back in Poland, back in the country from which we had escaped a year before.

Immediately our armed guards took up positions on the platform. The locomotive was uncoupled and left to take on water, and after a while returned. The soldiers settled back in their positions and with a piercing whistle the engine set off again.

For a while we travelled fast for a cattle train, the telegraph poles along the track whipping by like little blows on my eyes. I felt a hand on my shoulder. It was my father. His face was gloomy and his bushy eyebrows furrowed, his lips tightened. Little Mara switched her position and came out of her mother's arms into her father's, as if a man, her father, the head of all the kumpania, could save her and all of us. "Is this the end?" I asked soberly. I could not help cherishing reverence for my father, his leadership and his wisdom.

175

He shrugged. "Maybe," he said. "And maybe not." He even managed a smile. "It's like the Red Sea. Most of Pharaoh's Gypsies perished, but some survived. It is important that some survive. Because then our nation will live."

I gave up my place at the truck's opening to my father, so that he could rest his eyes on the fields, green again in the spring.

I looked around at the dirty sweaty people, hungry and exhausted, so full of joy only yesterday morning, so wretched and miserable now. This is how the Kelderari must have looked when taken out of the Brest Litovsk ghetto; this was how the Lowari felt when they were brought to dig their own mass grave on the road to Lukov, or the Bergitka Roma, caught at the Hungarian border. I was dazed, as though I could not understand that we were to share their fate. Somewhere in me there was a streak of defiance, perhaps inherited from my father, or perhaps imbued in me by my carefree schooldays in Poland, or possibly hardened by our trek to Hungary, with its endless perils that we finally managed to overcome. I could not see now what was going on outside. My father was at the ventilation slat. At the other end was Franko Zbar, his round and blotched face filling it entirely.

"I can see crocuses," my father said. "Whole clusters of yellow and purple crocuses." A dreamlike smile lit his eyes momentarily, but then it vanished as his mind snapped back to reality. People in our truck swayed as our train changed rails again before easing out among drab brick tenement houses and arriving at a station building with the sign 'Bielsko-Biała'. "We are in Upper Silesia," my father said. "Not far from Cracow."

The soldiers escorting us did not leave their places and a minute later we started again. We were leaving the town and running alongside a main road and a green meadow beyond it, with cows slowly chewing the cud and raising their heads with indifferent wonder at the passing train.

176

"Look!" my father suddenly exclaimed, pointing at a road sign, but it passed us too fast. "It read," my father said, " 'Auschwitz' in German and beneath 'Oświęcim' in Polish – 20 kilometres." He sighed deeply. I felt a lump in my throat as my eyes lingered on the faces of my family, unaware that we were coming to our final destination.

After a while the road swung away from us, another line appeared alongside ours and then, unexpectedly and with a sharp jolt, the train came to a halt. My father stuck his head out as far as he could, looking to right and left. "We are in the middle of nowhere," he said. Over his shoulder I could see a small field and behind it a wood, a white hut gleaming through the trees. A large kerchiefed peasant woman was working some distance away, breaking the earth with her hoe. My father turned brusquely, casting a reflective glance on Mara, now calm, holding her mother's hand. His eyes narrowed, his breath was laboured. But then he heard voices outside and swung back to the truck's opening. The German guards were outside the train. They looked tired, their helmets tipped forward over their noses, their rifles held limply in the crooks of their arms, as they ambled about on the line and among the small bushes that hugged the railway, leisurely smoking and talking to each other. We heard a rattle of wheels approaching. The soldiers looked up towards the front of our train, where the double tracks were merged once again into a single track, then those who were standing on the rails moved away. The sound of the approaching train grew louder, then, just as its engine almost hit ours, it veered away on to the branch line. It ran slowly past our train, pulling cattle trucks with Stars of David and the word 'Juden' chalked on, just like ours, but although the doors were partly ajar, no faces were visible at the ventilation slats, and no soldiers rode on the running boards. The train had, no doubt, discharged its passengers.

Father and I exchanged dejected looks. Our locomotive gave out a shrill whistle, summoning the German soldiers back on board. Our truck jolted. Suddenly my father turned to Mara, grabbed her and lifted her in his arms. "What are you doing?" my mother screamed. Terrified, the girl threw her little arms around my father's neck, trying desperately to cling to him and kicking her legs against the wall as he strove to straighten them with his hand and to push them out of the car.

"No, no!" she sobbed hysterically. I was paralysed, unable to say or do anything.

The wheels were moving. "Hide in the bushes," my father ordered, "until our train disappears, then run to that woman and ask her to take you in!"

Then Mother understood. "Yes, Mara!" she cried out. "Do as Father says. We shall return for you!" she lied. She had no time to kiss her daughter; her lips just brushed the air as my sister now obediently let my father squeeze her tiny body out of the truck, her legs dangling in the air. The train was moving quicker now. My father slid Mara down as far as he could towards the ground, then let her slip out of his arms. She fell, turning over. I could not see whether she had hurt herself, but I caught a glimpse of her lifting her little face to look after us and then dashing behind a bush as she had been told. Our truck was the last of all the trucks, our ventilation slat the last in the train. Miraculously, none of the soldiers noticed anything. I could not see my sister any longer, but in the distance the Polish peasant woman had stopped hoeing and was walking forward towards her.

My mother threw herself into my father's arms, weeping. As I brokenly tried to lend him support, she pulled out from her bodice the chain with the medallion of the Black Madonna and began to pray for the safety of her daughter.

My grandparents, my wife, the others, still stunned, just gaped at us, as our train passed a town without stopping. Then it crossed a very broad river, no doubt the Vistula, and began to slow down.

In front of us I could see row after row of barracks behind

wide ditches and triple barbed wire with numerous watch-towers, the tallest of which loomed in front of us, rising above a gateway between two large buildings. On the gate was an arched metalwork sign, 'Arbeit Macht Frei' – 'Work Frees You'.

Incredibly, I could hear music. When our train pulled to a stop at a large railway ramp, not only were there German officers and soldiers waiting, but also an orchestra. The prisoners' band, dressed in striped pyjama-like clothes, was playing a lusty Strauss waltz to welcome us to Auschwitz.

2

The doors of all the cattle trucks in front of ours were unbolted by armed SS men who were holding German shepherd dogs on leashes. From our ventilation slat I watched the Jews being ordered out, and those who moved too slowly were helped down the planks by a rifle butt or a snarling attack from one of the dogs.

People lined up, women holding babies in their arms, men and children carrying battered valises or bundles. "Why are they keeping us in the truck?" Franko Zbar asked worriedly. My father kept silent. He and I, glued to our observation spots, watched with apprehension what was happening. A German officer, followed by his aides, was walking alongside the Jews and with a thumb pointing to the left or the right. Soldiers immediately shoved the people to the side directed by their superior. All the old people, those who looked ill, and small children were being sent to the left. There were desperate cries as families were separated. I saw one woman, sent to the right, bolting out of her line and joining her little girl on the left. An SS guard tried to push her away. "I don't want to live any longer!" the woman shouted, clinging to the sobbing child, its little arms clutching her mother's neck. Magnanimously the SS officer waved the guard off. "Lassen sie da! Leave her there!"

Suddenly our door was flung open. The SS men shouted, "Raus, Zigeuner!" A plank was thrown down and we descended, all of us, our dark Gypsy faces ashen from fear in the broad daylight. The thick stench of unwashed human bodies and sweat wafted sourly in the air.

Two trucks were coming towards us. The soldiers ordered us to climb on to the vehicles. A young SS lieutenant asked who our leader was. "I am," my father answered in German.

"You are going to Zigeunerlager," the officer said. "The Gypsy camp, the family camp. You'll like it there."

"What will happen to us?" my father's voice wavered.

"What do you mean? Nothing. You are not Jews, you are Aryans, like us." These were exactly the words that Colonel Krüger had uttered in Brest Litovsk at Mikita Kowal's birthday party.

"But this is a . . . concentration camp." I knew from the pause my father made that he wanted to say a different word, perhaps 'extermination', but thought better of it.

"You'll work. We need all the manpower we can get, to help us in our effort to crush the Bolsheviks." Again the familiar words of Colonel Krüger. "In that camp you'll find Sintis, some of them officers and soldiers of the Wehrmacht." He smiled indulgently, keeping up the conversation as a few of the soldiers boarded the vehicles with us and the others closed up the rear. "Gute Reise!" he added. "Have a good journey!"

Where were we going? I wondered. Suddenly the spirits of those around me rose. Auschwitz had been just a stop on our way, to discharge the Jews. People need to believe in the best, not the worst. The men of our kumpania had not seen the execution of the Gypsies on the road to Lukov, had not seen the flames of Sobibor as I had.

The trucks started. We drove on a road alongside a branch railway line that was being built, with scores of men working on it in the striped uniforms of the camp. On our right stretched a forest, with farmhouses dotting its edges. The countryside waking up to the spring looked peaceful and pastoral – contrasting sharply with the emaciated band from the camp working on our left. All the time, preoccupied with what was happening to us, I scarcely felt Zoya's hand in mine. But now I squeezed it with feigned reassurance, before I looked at my father, an old habit, one of eighteen years. His face remained grim in spite of what he had heard from the SS lieutenant. I turned to my mother. She was drying the tears which she had shed for my sister. "We shall find her," I said to her, leaning forward and kissing her cheek. "When the war is over." My voice trailed off. I could hardly believe what I was saying.

Abruptly the barbed wire and the watch-towers on the left of our road came to an end. The people in my truck smiled with relief. Even when a new camp and new barbed wire came into view, their mood did not change. "This is the other camp – for us," my grandfather Sandu said. "A work camp."

We passed through a gate with armed sentries guarding the entrance. A huge complex of wooden barracks with a few brick buildings stretched in front of us. "Birkenau," an SS man explained helpfully. We rode past a men's camp and a women's camp, but as I saw that the prisoners had the Star of David sewn on to their jackets, a cold shiver ran down my spine. We *were* in another camp, but Jews were there, too. And where there were Jews, nothing good could be in store for us. The German lieutenant had deceived us. But then suddenly another part of the camp came into view. Incredibly, I saw groups of old women chatting among themselves, old men smoking pipes or playing harmonicas, children dancing and laughing. Everyone around me was peering out eagerly. "They are our people!" Gregory Mular shouted jubilantly. Gypsies in the camp waved to us.

"The officer did not lie!" my grandfather said spiritedly.

We stopped at the last barrack. "Sauna!" the SS guard volunteered. "Entlausung – disinfection!"

From the barrack a fatherly-looking SS sergeant rushed out to meet us. "Only the men may come down!" he shouted. "Women wait!" As we began to climb down from the truck, he added reassuringly, "You're dirty after the trip. You'll take showers and change your clothes." Again I looked at my father. He nodded slightly as if agreeing with the sergeant. I turned to Zoya still on the truck, her eyes following me, and gave her a nod like my father had done.

We trudged into the building. There was a long table manned by Gypsy prisoners in blue and white striped trousers and jackets, supervised by SS guards. "Undress!" the sergeant ordered. "And hand over your clothes." We did as instructed, one after another handing over what we had. I tried to keep my gold watch, but the sergeant said, "Everything! You must keep nothing. It will be given back to you!" The prisoner behind the table asked in perfect German, "What's your name?" He must be a Sinti, I decided. I answered and saw him scribbling my name on a tag and pinning it to my clothes. My father held his fiddle tight to himself. "It will be given back to you," the SS guard said to him. "All Gypsies get their instruments back. Get into the sauna."

But the next room to which we were sent, naked as the day we were born, was not the sauna. I saw several Jewish prisoners here, each behind a chair, each holding hair-clippers in his hand. I sat between my father and my uncle Rudolf. The prisoners, I guessed, were professional barbers, brought from another part of the camp for the occasion. They all looked very thin, their bones pro-truding, their eyes sunk deep, wearing a perennially sad, resigned expression. My hair was being swiftly cut off, and I watched it falling down, the only blond locks on the floor among dark Gypsy hair. "Ready?" the SS guard asked me. "Go, take a shower!" He pointed at a door, in front of which I noticed another Jewish prisoner with a huge pile of towels and a basin filled with cakes of soap. I was handed a bar and a towel and passed through the door.

I saw several rows of showers. "Hell!" I heard Franko Zbar hiss his disgust. "When I wash, I feel dirty. I no longer feel like a man." But in he went and so did all of us. For me it was not a problem. I had always taken showers in Warsaw. The water was icy cold. I dried myself and came out. Our clothes had already gone; the hair, swept up from the floor, was being packed into sacks. Three sacks bore labels in German, 'Foreign currency', 'Jewellery', 'Watches'. My heart turned over. I was certain my gold watch was in that last sack.

The same prisoners we had seen before had striped uniforms ready piled up for us on the table. Each of us was handed a set and also a pair of wooden shoes picked up from baskets on the floor. "I have two left ones," I heard Antoni Puma complain. "Mine are too big," Bora Natkin protested. "Mine too small," Leon Kwiatek said. "This is not a shoe shop," the SS sergeant intervened. "No exchange is allowed. Be quick, your ladies are waiting."

We were led out of the back door and, slushing through the mud, reached an alleyway running parallel to the main one. We could not see our women, nor they us. With a heavy heart I thought of my wife's beautiful long raven hair about to land on the floor, put into a sack, and then probably taken by train on the way to Germany. I hardly noticed I was entering a barrack or being ushered to a long table behind which sat another group of Sinti prisoners, again under the supervision of SS guards. "Stand in line!" an SS man said. I could no longer see the sergeant. He had apparently chosen to stay with the women.

We formed a queue. While my father-in-law and my uncle were exchanging their shoes behind me, I heard a guard ordering, "Bare your arms!" I did not understand why, but the first of the prisoners behind the table was dipping a needle into an inkpot and tattooing the capital letter 'Z' and a four-digit number on my father's forearm.

When my turn came I was passed on to another man who opened a folder and wrote on top of it, 'Auschwitz II-BII E'. Birkenau, I realised, was part of the big Auschwitz complex of camps. The man was filling in the questionnaire with the answers to my name, age, place of birth, tribe and other particulars. He wrote German and spoke German.

184

When our registration was over, we were all taken to another barrack. The SS sergeant was coming across the camp towards us. "This is where you'll live," he said amiably. "Welcome! By the way, my name is Otto Fürst. This barrack is mine."

We entered. The place was partly filled with Gypsies, old people and children, the latter wearing oversized adult camp clothing with sleeves that hid their hands, and trousers that swept the floor. They all surged towards us, talking at once in Polish, Czech, German and various Romany dialects.

"Stand back!" The sergeant raised his hand to them. "Let the new arrivals settle first, you can talk later." I saw bunks with straw mattresses and a single blanket, three in a group, one on top of another, awaiting us. The barrack had two doors, on its left and right, a tall stove, and two tables in the middle where, surprisingly, stood vases with fresh-cut flowers. "From our own nurseries," the sergeant said. "Welcome!" Then he amiably patted the head of one of our little boys who had just taken off his huge jacket, trying to figure out how to shorten it. "Hey, where is your number?" the sergeant asked. The boy pulled down his trousers and showed his little buttocks and the number tattooed there. His forearm had been too narrow to accommodate the letter and four digits.

Some of the men burst out laughing, which the sergeant chose to ignore, but at this moment our women entered. They wore prisoners' striped uniforms and their heads were shaven. My eyes darted towards Zoya. She was trying to hide the crown of her head with her hand, and so was my mother who was right behind her. My heart went out to them both. My father closed his eyes tight as if he could not bear the humiliation.

Exhausted from the ordeal, we all lay down. Our family took one triple-tier bunk, each narrow bed for two people. My grandparents took the bottom bunk closest to the floor, my parents the middle one and Zoya and I had the top one.

185

We had to climb up, but at least we also had most of the fresh air from the cracks in the roof.

"I'm sorry," my wife said.

"Sorry for what?"

"My hair." She kept her distance, unsure of my reaction, her hands still trying to cover her bare head.

"My God!" I said and took her into my arms. "I love you, for yourself, not for your looks." She burst into uncontrollable crying. "I mean," I added quickly, "it doesn't matter, your hair, besides it will grow back. Haven't you seen the others? They allow the hair to grow back. They shave it just the one time, for hygiene."

"How long will it take? For my hair to grow back."

My lovely Zoya. All she was concerned about in this concentration camp was her looks, so that she could again be her beautiful self for her husband. "A few months."

"I must get a scarf," she said. "From somewhere, but I must."

Suddenly a gong sounded. A large container was being wheeled in by other Gypsy prisoners. "Come and eat!" they shouted in Polish. We clambered down. There was now a stack of tin cups and plates and aluminium cutlery on the table. Sergeant Fürst was in charge. "Take a set," he ordered, "and keep them. Remember, it's the property of the Third Reich. Don't lose them. Get in line."

We did so. We got real Gypsy soup made from nettles, and bread. Our family shared a whole loaf – part oats, part potatoes, part sawdust. The soup was good and warm and we did not mind what the bread was made from. This was to be our daily bread from now on, to fill our empty stomachs, and we blessed the heavens for it.

Although it was daytime, we settled down on our bunks to get some sleep after all the time and travelling since being caught on the road in Hungary. Zoya, more confidently, cuddled into my shoulder and, when I kissed her, she eagerly, as if almost disbelieving it, smothered me passionately with kisses. I made love to her, not because I

186

really felt like it or had a strength to, but because it was the only thing I could do to convince her that I loved her even without her hair, and at the same time to reassure ourselves that we were both alive in Auschwitz.

Later in the afternoon we were awakened by the gong. Sergeant Fürst and the SS guards were calling us to get into line. They were being helped by some Sinti kapos who were better treated than anyone else because they assisted the Nazis. Across the same muddy ground we were marched to the same barrack where we had been tattooed and had had files opened on us.

This time three officers were sitting behind the table, our documents in front of them. They began assigning jobs – young men to laying water pipes in the hard ground, young women to levelling muddy ground. Those who were past middle age were directed to cleaning latrines or to carrying the food containers. Like all the families we stood together, my parents, grandparents, Zoya and I. I noticed that one of the officers was dressed differently from the others. He wore jodhpur boots and white gloves, as if he had been called on duty just before going out riding.

Slowly our turn came. The officer wearing the gloves picked up my father's file, then looked up, his eyes squinting as if searching his memory. What struck me about him was not just his swarthy, almost Gypsylike complexion, but a large cleft between his upper teeth that somehow looked familiar. The German raised his forefinger. "I know you," he said, pointing it at my father.

A flash of recognition dawned on my father and me at the same time. "Fukier's Wine Cellar," my father said.

"Of course! In Warsaw Old Town."

"You asked me to play Brahms and Liszt. You're a doctor, from Bavaria."

"Correct! Doktor Josef Mengele. Do you have your fiddle with you?"

"They took it away in the sauna."

"You'll get it back. Immediately!" Excitedly the officer leaned towards the one sitting next to him and whispered something in German that we could not hear. His colleague nodded approval. "You'll play in a Gypsy orchestra," Mengele said.

"Orchestra?" my father asked, bewildered.

"Of course. What kind of a Gypsy camp would it be without an orchestra?"

He quickly made a note on my father's file and the captain next to him, apparently the head of the commission, signed it 'Hauptsturmbannführer Perry Board'. Dr Mengele added his signature, 'Hauptsturmbannführer Doktor Josef Mengele'.

"My son, my wife, you remember them?" Father said. "They were playing with me that same night at Fukier's. And my daughter-in-law, she is a dancer, a very good dancer."

"It's a string orchestra," Mengele said. "And you're the only one of your family who plays violin. Remember, I invited you to come to my home-town for an engagement?" He chuckled. "Well, I have kept my promise. Auschwitz is now my home-town." Again he consulted his colleagues, then looked at the files. "Your women will get jobs in the kitchen – your parents won't work – too old. As for the young man, well, he looks good and strong . . ."

"My son finished high school in Warsaw," my father said quickly. "He speaks perfect German."

"So do all the Sinti."

"But they don't speak Polish. He speaks perfect Polish, too."

"Dolmetscher, eh? Translator. Well, we do have a number of Polish Gypsies here . . ." He pointed again with his finger. "Because you are an artist, who plays real Gypsy music, and because he is your son, I will take him to my office. As Dolmetscher he will be useful."

"Thank you, sir," my father said and gave me a nudge.

"Thank you," I repeated.

188

We walked out of the barrack. Almost immediately some of the Elders who were in our barrack before us, joined us and began asking where we came from. Were there still Gypsies travelling the roads? What was happening at the front? However, we were even more eager than they to ask questions, to find out about the camp. Most of them came from Poland, from the Białystok area. They had been here for months. Only recently, they said, had they been given striped camp uniforms; before that they had worn their own clothes. There had also been a canteen where they could buy cigarettes, sausage, razor blades. But their money had been taken from them, for their own protection. Gypsies steal even from Gypsies, they had said. And then of course they closed the canteen.

"How many people are in the Zigeunerlager?" my father asked.

"Six thousand at present. Some have been sent to other camps. Still, life is bearable. In the other parts of the camp, where the Jews are, there is only one end in sight. Some SS men joke that they come here through the gate and get out through the chimneys. The chimneys of the crematoria."

"Where are the crematoria?"

"There," an old man with a wizened face pointed. "Among the trees. Four brick buildings, three hundred metres behind you."

"I don't see any smoke coming out of the chimneys."

"Closed for repairs. Just for a day or two."

Suddenly my father took a step forward. "That man there, isn't that Janusz Kwiek, king of the Kelderari?"

"Yes," a number of people answered at once. My father shook his head painfully. I looked at the stooped old man surrounded by others, standing in a group. He felt my father's glance on him and came forward.

"Are you Kelderari, the group that came in today?"

"No, we are Polska Roma, the Lowland Gypsies. But I played at your coronation in Warsaw. I played violin."

The old man waved his hand. "Just a memory."

189

"It was a splendid affair. The Polish primate, the archbishop of Gniezno, anointed your Majesty. And I remember your speech. You said," my father talked excitedly, "that it is our duty to educate our sons and daughters, so that one day the Gypsy nation may take its rightful place as a member of the League of Nations."

Kwiek smiled. "July 4, 1937. Only seven years ago. Seems an eternity. Are there any Gypsies free outside?"

"Oh, yes. In Hungary, at least."

"Not for long, not for long." He looked at me and Zoya. "Sooner or later we will share the fate of the Jews. But you, you younger ones, try to escape if you can. Save yourselves. Have children and educate them." He blinked his eyes, then rubbed them. "I'm tired, I must lie down."

And he walked away. We watched in silence as the lonely, bent figure of the king of the Gypsies, in the striped uniform of the camp, receded into the distance on the Lagerstrasse of Auschwitz.

3

The bugle sounded at 6 a.m. We all gathered at the Appell-platz, a sea of Gypsies on a huge barren square divided into groups by barracks, and our names were called out by the SS men in charge, before we were sent out to work. When I trudged through the mud to Dr Mengele's office, there were a number of children there under the supervision of two guards. I had a long time to wait, but finally at eight o'clock Dr Mengele arrived, accompanied by a fat blonde German nurse in uniform. This time he was dressed in smartly creased regulation SS uniform and shining boots. He put on a doctor's white overall, picked up a magnifying glass and bent over the children. One after another he lifted their eyelids to examine their eyeballs. He selected a pair of twin girls, their bared numbers tattooed with ZW, for Zwillings – twins – above their camp number. He asked them some questions. They answered in Polish. "Where is that Dolmetscher? Oh, there you are. What's your name?" I told him. "Right, the son of the artist." He turned to the nurse. "Get him some paper and a pencil. He writes." Then he addressed me again. "Ask those children their names, where and when they were born and to what tribe they belong." I took down the information. "Light brown eyes," the doctor said. "Be sure you write 'light brown', not 'brown'." Then he told the nurse, "Transcribe the informa-tion from his notes into your book. Weigh the girls and measure their height as usual. Then give them injections. Same dose as given to the others. One a day. I want to see them again in ten days."

191

As a guard led the children out, I could hear the rumble of motor vehicles. Through the open door I caught a glimpse of trucks passing by, packed with emaciated Jewish men, women and children, escorted by armed soldiers. They were being driven along the Lagerstrasse in the direction of the brick buildings in full view of the Gypsies.

"Dolmetscher!" I heard the by now familiar voice. "Come with me. We're going to the hospital."

I followed Mengele out of his office and then to a huge barrack complex nearby surrounded by barbed wire, with guards posted at the entrance. In the first barrack Gypsy women were lying on the rows of three-tiered bunks, most of them naked, their skin covered with infected scurvy sores, their weight shrunk to half of their normal weight. Among them moved white-coated men, stethoscopes hanging from their necks, some examining patients, others giving directions to the nurses. At the sight of Dr Mengele they quickly gathered around him. "Ten died last night," one of them reported. "From gangrene. We are running out of medicine. We need vitamins – vitamin C especially."

Mengele shrugged. "Take the best care of them you can, Pfleger," he said. He moved on to a young pretty woman lying on the lowest bunk, her face still unscarred by sores, and asked her a question. She answered in a Romany dialect. Mengele beckoned to me. "Ask her where her wounds are?" I did so. The woman opened her long night-shirt to show her chest. Most of the skin there was gone, revealing bare red flesh.

As the doctor went on looking at his patients, I asked one of the Polish doctors, "Why does he call you all 'Pfleger' – 'male nurse'?"

"Only an Aryan can be a doctor," the man answered. "We are Jewish."

We went on to the next barrack which was filled with male typhus patients, then the next, reserved for those with dysentery and chronic diarrhoea, and after that to one

192

filled only with children and youngsters. A terrible stench permeated the air. The patients had mouths infested with ulcers, inside and outside. Some also had cheeks perforated by their illness, the most sickening sight I had ever seen.

"Are you giving vitamins to them, Epstein?" Mengele asked the middle-aged man in charge of the barrack.

"Yes, Doctor."

"Good."

"Ask this girl," Mengele said to me when Epstein was called to a patient, "whether she gets vitamin pills." The girl confirmed it. Mengele wanted to be sure that the Jewish doctors gave pills to the sick and did not steal them for themselves. It was different here, I noticed, compared to the scurvy department; vitamins were available here. When Epstein returned, Mengele said, as if explaining his decision, "I am especially interested in noma. I may even write a scientific paper on it. I want everyone here to be well treated."

"I know, I'm doing my best."

"Any case of recovery?"

"No, Doctor, not one so far."

There were many other barracks in the hospital camp, but at this point Mengele decided to leave off his inspection.

It was when we returned to his office that I suddenly heard the music. In the distance violins were playing 'The Blue Danube'. Through an open window came the smouldering stench of roasting meat. Mengele himself shut the door angrily. I looked out and saw the chimneys of the brick buildings belching forth huge streaks of flame and smoke. Just like in Sobibor. It was from over there that the sound of the violins was coming. It was intended to calm the Jews going inside, soap and towels in their hands, no doubt believing they were taking a bath. Except that it was not a bath-house, but a crematorium. The Gypsy orchestra was there, my father was there, their music

193

helping to make a smooth transition for the Jews from life to death.

It was April 20, 1944, Hitler's birthday. Swastika flags were hanging from all over the camp. Everybody was free from work and extra rations of bread and soup and even a few festive slices of sausage were issued. The Gypsy musicians played all the time. The Jewish painters, who had come from outside, had completed painting the school barrack which now had a sign but no pupils, and instead had been turned into a Kindergarten, with a real merry-go-round, which opened on the Führer's birthday. Children rode on wooden horses, laughing happily, while others played hop-scotch, or hide-and-seek. I saw Irina, with her little boy weeping unconsolably. "Why are you crying, Puji?" I asked. The child pointed to a picture of a lovely green hill, with trees and a cow, painted on the barrack wall and burst into a new fit of sobbing. He could remember the outside world, I guessed. Birkenau had only mud and clay, not a blade of grass.

At noon, accompanied by several officers, Dr Mengele appeared in the camp. Children ran to him, shouting, "Uncle Mengele! Uncle Mengele!" He dug into his pockets and threw them some sweets. "Dance, dance!" he encouraged them. He smiled at a few pretty girls, inspected the Kindergarten, talked to the German women assigned to it, and then joined the head of the Political Department of Birkenau, American-born SS Captain Perry Board, as well as other officers on a specially erected platform. We, the Gypsies, lined up on both sides of the road.

The orchestra broke into a march and the parade began. Some two hundred men were walking towards us in military formation, four abreast, an entire company in the striped uniforms of the camp, with wartime decorations, even a few Iron Crosses, pinned to the ex-soldiers' chests for the occasion. These were the Sinti, the German Gypsies taken away from the Eastern Front and sent to Auschwitz.

As they were approaching, I could hear their marching song:

Wir standen für Deutschland
auf Posten and hielten die heilige Wacht.
Führer, befiehl, wir folgen dir!

The officers raised their arms in salute, as the Gypsy Wehrmacht veterans, eyes right to the platform, goose-stepped by, singing, at the tops of their voices, their obedience to the Führer on the Führer's birthday.

Where I worked, in Dr Mengele's office, often making hospital rounds with him, was another world – a world of spot fever and scarlet fever, typhoid and dysentery, tuberculosis and noma, and smallpox or varieties of scurvy which inevitably led to gangrene and death. Here the Gypsies were dying by hundreds every day. This, I understood from overhearing exchanges between the SS guards and the blonde nurse, was our destiny. Not to be gassed or burned like Jews. We were Aryans, as Colonel Krüger and the lieutenant who welcomed us to Auschwitz had said, and were not destined for a crematorium. Being asocial elements, we had to die of 'natural causes'.

The Gypsies in the camp, those outside the hospital, had a childlike mentality. The young worked hard, but even they believed that they would get through the war. A Gypsy can cry for himself, but he will never lose hope, never lose his song. This has helped us to survive through thousands of years. Our Aryan origin was our insurance – no crematorium for us, starvation yes, but even this did not deter our people from playing, singing and dancing in Auschwitz. Meanwhile, we were all losing weight. On 150 grams of bread a day, a bowl of nettle soup, a black acorn-scented liquid which the Germans called coffee, a small spoonful of beet marmalade or margarine, and only on Sundays pea or fish-powder soup, we had no protein, no fat, no vitamins to sustain us for long. "Well," the Gypsies kept saying

195

hopefully, "we are starving, but at least we are starving together."

In May more Gypsies arrived and the population of the camp swelled to some 8,000. There were no spare barracks, so we slept twelve where at first six had been supposed to lie, and when the number increased further, we slept by shifts. Then we traded – a slice of bread for an hour of sleep. I watched my beloved wife getting thinner by the day and there was little I could do to help. I watched my mother and my grandparents fading and I could do nothing. Only my father looked healthy. The orchestra members had special rations, even schnaps, but the SS guards and the kapos made sure that they consumed everything they got on the spot, so that nothing was smuggled back to the camp. We never talked about what he saw during his work; he was under penalty of death not to speak about it, but I had no need to be told. Day after day we watched, night after night we listened to, the never-ending truckloads of Jews being driven openly through our camp to the crematoria, skeletons already even before they were gassed and burned. Each column had some twenty trucks, each with fifty people packed like sardines in a can. Between five thousand and ten thousand Jews passed each day, never to return. The same trucks were driven back containing sacks full of hair, gold teeth, underwear. The chimneys worked unceasingly and the orchestra played as every batch came in, half of the musicians during the daytime, half at night.

By June the benevolent attitude of SS officers and guards towards us had undergone a marked change. When we gathered for roll-call at 6 a.m. and 6 p.m. at the Appellplatz, we often had to witness someone being given twenty-five lashes for the slightest infringement of the rules. A father once threw some bread to his child across the Kindergarten fence, and an SS guard shot the child right on the spot, to penalise the father. Then they turned the Kindergarten into an orphanage, no longer cared for by the German women,

196

but by Gypsy ones. With so many people dying, there were hundreds of orphaned children. Except for my grandfather, father and Gregory Mular, all the members of our Council of Elders had died, either of typhus or of pneumonia. There were rumours that half a million Hungarian Jews were being transported to Auschwitz and that we might soon have to make room for them. My grandfather never lost his optimism. "It's better than *that*," he would say, pointing at the smoking chimneys. "We live, our entire family is alive . . . One must bear it all in silence. One musn't scratch where it doesn't itch." My father said nothing, but after a while he took me aside and said, "Roman, you must escape. And you must remember it all and write it down for the world to know, to make sure that it will never happen again."

"Father," I said, "we have been here three months and not a single Gypsy has been gassed."

My father closed his eyes. He swallowed painfully and I saw the dimple on his chin covered by a film of sweat. "Do you think the Nazis would murder all the Jews," he said, "and leave us alive as witnesses, unless they knew that in the end there would be no witnesses?"

Almost every evening Dr Mengele used to ride around the camp on his horse, because, as he told me once, he had loved its lights, our music and songs ever since his childhood when Gypsy caravans used to come to his Bavarian town. Once he rode with the tall dark-haired commandant of the whole Auschwitz camp, Colonel Rudolf Hoess, who had a white stallion and who chain-smoked even while riding. Mengele ordered Sergeant Fürst to wake up my father. "This is the artist," he introduced him to Hoess. "Play, Gypsy, play now for the commandant – Brahms, Liszt or Bartok."

And my father played. In the hushed stillness of Birkenau after the daytime transports had finished and before the night ones began, his violin solos echoed across the camp, not only for the Nazis, but also for all the

197

Gypsies, because he knew that they were listening – the Kelderari king, Janusz Kwiek; the Gypsy noblemen, the Majewskis and the Sadowskis; the Polska Roma and Bergitka Roma, the Kelderari, the Lowari, the Sinti. They were all listening, and his music gave them strength to go on and to hope against hope that they would survive.

Lila and Tala, the twins I met at my first visit to Dr Mengele's office, were being examined by him. "Nu, wunderbar!" he exclaimed. He turned to all of us, the nurse and me and the SS guards, in a jubilant mood. "They *are* lighter! Not yet blue, but definitely lighter. Who knows, maybe I shall manage to turn those twins into full-blooded Aryans! Bring them back in ten days' time." The girls were taken to BIIF Ward, which was not in our camp, but a special Gypsy division for the study of twins in the general male hospital of Birkenau.

Mengele went on to other children. He compared their hair to a palette of hair samples which he held in his hand, and dictated the appropriate number to the nurse. After that she weighed them and took them to a wall where there were already numerous nails marking their height, and chalked their names next to a new nail she would hammer in. If they grew taller they would get sweets; if not, they would be sent to the Gypsy orphanage even though they were not orphans.

"Come!" Mengele said to me. "Our weekly tour of the hospital." Outside it was getting calmer. All day there had been storms with lightning and thunder but the rain had now settled into a steady drizzle. I followed Mengele with a pencil and notepad. I was now his special assistant – taking notes in German, Polish and Romany and then passing them to him directly upon our return to the office. I often got praise from him, but not extra food. Only once did I ask for it, for Zoya, and he yelled that if I mentioned it once more he would have me put on hard labour.

There was no tour of the hospital barrack where by now

a thousand Gypsies lay sick and dying. Mengele went straight to the noma department, the Nomaabteilung, the area of his special interest, where some seventy youngsters lay in three-tiered bunks. For some reason noma did not attack adults. Again Mengele talked to some of the patients, more often than not through me, as they were either Polish or Czech, which I understood easily because of its similarity to Polish. Then he found Dr Epstein and beckoned to him. They went to Epstein's office, a small partition in the barrack, and were closeted there for a quarter of an hour before Mengele came out. "Remember, Professor," I heard him say at the door; this was the first time he called the Jewish doctor not 'Pfleger' or even 'Doctor', but by his academic title. "You get everything you want for your patients, I get the paper in a month's time."

As Mengele moved on, I heard Professor Epstein, red-faced, talking to his Czech colleague. He had forgotten that I understood most if not every word. "He has offered to prolong my life. Mind you, not to save it, just to prolong it, if I prepare a scientific paper on noma, which he would publish under his own name. It will keep him away from the front, he said, and justify his presence here as a scientist."

"Come here!" I heard Mengele call. He had been looking at a bunk where an eight-year-old girl, alive half an hour ago, now lay immobile and lifeless. "I want an autopsy on this girl."

"Jawohl, Herr Doktor," Professor Epstein said, and then added to his colleague with a smile, "but in return he gives me everything we need for the patients – sulphonamides, vitamins, fresh meat and vegetables."

It was almost six o'clock. As I did not have time to get back to my barrack, I ran straight to the Appellplatz to join the others for roll-call. An elderly man was bent over, receiving twenty-five lashes, and worse, having to count them for the guidance of the SS man administering the punishment. His striped camp trousers were torn and blood

199

oozed from the cuts on his buttocks. The man raised his face and I recognised, in spite of its expression of pain and humiliation, the noble features of the king of the Kelderari, Janusz Kwiek. "God in heaven!" my father uttered, grief-stricken. He was probably remembering it all – the coronation, the presence of the primate of Poland, and the king's address to his people. Gregory Mular whispered to me that Kwiek had been denounced by a kapo for telling the Gypsies to start hiding knives and razors for a possible confrontation with the Nazis if and when they, too, were taken to the crematoria.

Sergeant Fürst began counting the people of our barrack. "One is missing," he said.

"Yes," my father answered. "My mother. She was taken ill suddenly."

When we returned to the barrack, I rushed to my grandmother. She was lying on the lowest bunk. My grandfather sat by her, helplessly holding her hand. Others gathered around her. "How are you feeling?" my father asked. He turned to me. "She was all right two hours ago." This week my father was on the night shift and free in the daytime. He sighed deeply. "We'd better get her to the hospital," he said after a while.

My grandmother heard him. Her wizened face tightened further, her lips were pale, only her forehead and her eyes burned from fever. "Don't," she whispered. "It's no use. I don't need any doctor to tell me that my time is up."

I wanted to rush her to the hospital, to get help, but my father stopped me. He did not cry. He had run out of tears in Auschwitz, even for his own mother. My grandmother raised her hand and touched his cheek, then mine, my mother's and Zoya's. Her eyes rested on her husband. "Sandu," she said. "Remember when we were married by the Polish priest in the church. On The Union of Lublin Street. It was the happiest day of my life. It was worth being born for it."

The moment she closed her eyes, I knew she was gone. I

don't know which of the numerous illnesses raging through our camp was responsible. All of our kumpania stood silent, paying their respect to a woman who had seen generations of Gypsies grow, had taught girls how to tell fortunes, had administered medicine like a real doctor, and who now, unable to do anything more for them, had taken her leave. I heard my grandfather mumbling to himself, his voice sinking. As our people were bidding farewell to their Pchuri Daj, I could still feel the touch of my grandmother's hand on my cheek.

4

On June 26, 1944, the sky over Auschwitz thundered and the wooden walls of the office barrack reverberated from the roar of engines. As we all ran out – Mengele, the nurse, other staff members and I – we caught glimpses of silver wings painted with stars and stripes and 'USAAF' signs. No sirens had time to sound, but anti-aircraft fire was responding to the American intrusion. I saw Professor Epstein rushing out from the nearby noma barrack, a valise in his hand. Mengele's standing orders were that, if the Allies bombed the camp, he must run out into the fields with all his scientific documents on noma.

Suddenly it was all over. The planes flew away. Perhaps it was just a reconnaissance, but they were bombers and they did not bomb the camp. They could have hit the crematoria and halted the murder of the innocents for quite a while. In the commotion some Jews and Gypsies could have escaped, and if, in addition, the railway lines leading to Auschwitz had been bombed, the transportation to the camp of Hungarian Jews, which had now begun, would also have been interrupted. I hope God has forgiven the generals who planned the flights without ever ordering the bombing of death-camp installations and the rails leading to it, because the survivors of Auschwitz, Jews and Gypsies alike, never did.

An hour after the raid, the twins, Lila and Tala, were brought in for their usual inspection. The nurse called Dr Mengele, who was pacing the floor, visibly shaken, furiously cursing the Americans. But as soon as he examined the

202

girls' eyes, his humour returned. "Wunderbar!" I heard him exclaim. "They are almost blue! Schwester!" he called the nurse. "I want their eyes preserved in flacons."

The fat woman asked matter-of-factly, "Phenolic acid or benzine?"

"Benzine," Mengele said.

The nurse sterilised a syringe, while the twins calmly looked at each other, expecting another injection aimed at changing the colour of their eyes. "Take them out," Mengele said, glancing at me. He smiled amiably at them.

An hour later the nurse brought to Mengele's office two flacons, each with a pair of eyeballs swimming in alcohol. Mengele picked up the flacons and looked at them in the light of the window. "Interessant," he said. "Sehr interessant!"

In those flacons was all that remained of the beautiful Gypsy twins.

When I returned to my barrack, still unable to dismiss the past day's experiences from my mind, I found my mother and my grandfather. In the distance I could hear the orchestra and knew that my father was there beyond the birch trees at the west end of the Birkenau camp where smoke was constantly rising from the crematoria.

"Zoya!" I called, but heard no answer. She normally worked with my mother; a week earlier they had both been switched from the kitchen to the much heavier work of lugging the heavy stones away from the camp's ground. "Where is Zoya?" I asked. Mother looked at me with a heavy sigh, but said nothing. My grandfather turned his gaunt face away. Then my mother put her arm around my shoulder and pulled me against her chest. "She is ill."

"Ill!" I screamed. "What is it? Dysentery, typhus?"

"We don't know," Mother said.

Without another word, I rushed out. It was time to go to

the Appellplatz to be counted, but instead I dashed back, my feet sinking in the mud on my way. The guards knew me; they let me pass. I went from barrack to barrack. She was not in the one marked with 'Achtung! Typhus!', nor in the dysentery, scurvy or pneumonia departments. Clenching my fists and feverishly whispering prayers, hoping against hope that she was not there, I entered the Nomaabteilung, from which so far not a single child or youngster had come out alive. I rushed among the tiers of bunks. "Are you looking for someone?" I heard Dr Epstein's voice. I did not answer, because at that very moment I saw her. I saw my Zoya, her growing hair still covered by a scarf, her face drenched in sweat, her sunken cheeks underlining her still-beautiful coal-black eyes. "Darling!" I shouted and threw myself on to her bunk. It took her a seemingly endless minute to recognise me. Then a faint smile appeared on her pale lips. "Roman," she said. "Roman!" She tried to lift her hand to touch my cheek, but it fell with no strength left in it.

Behind me Dr Epstein stopped. "Your wife?" he asked. "Sister?"

"Wife," I said.

"With the drugs and fresh food I get now we have already managed to improve the state of some of the noma patients," he said. "Don't give up hope. I shall do all I can to save her, I promise you, young man."

I paid no attention to Sergeant Fürst bawling me out for not appearing at roll-call, nor could I touch the slice of stale bread or drink the watery soup they brought us for supper. My father and mother tried to console me until they finally gave up and went to sleep. I lay on my bunk, unable to close my eyes. I loved Zoya more than anything in the world, more even than my parents. On the top bunk of an adjacent set, my aunt Irina, her husband Leon next to her, their Puji between them, tried to overcome the baby's weeping by softly singing the song of a camp poet:

Oh, Gypsies, Gypsies,
They drive us to work!
They don't give us bread
And drive us to work!

God, oh God, my God,
I can't get out of here!
All my youth is wasting,
I won't see the world any more.

There won't be me any more,
The Germans will murder me,
God, my God, I'm passing away,
I won't see the world any more.

She stopped chanting and I could hear only her strangled sobs. I wished I could cry too but, like my father, I was no longer able. My aunt cried for me, cried for all of us as she finished her lullaby, the strangest of lullabies ever sung by a mother to her child.

There was a small celebration next morning. The work on connecting running water to Birkenau had at last been completed, and no longer would we have to drink and wash from the same tin bowl. Spigots appeared outside the barracks and people splashed themselves and each other until the SS guards stopped them, admonishing them not to waste precious water. Those who rejoiced had picked desperately on some pleasure with which to celebrate life as long as it lasted.

I stood outside my barrack, unwilling to wash, or to eat, when a container was brought in with a liquid which in colour only resembled coffee. "Roman, please!" My mother was trying to take me into her arms, as if I were still a boy. "Eat something. I saved your slice of bread from yesterday. And mine." Then Father talked to me, wisely as always, about my duties to myself and Zoya and how important it was for me not to give in.

"I hope Mara is alive and safe," Mother said suddenly. It was the first time in weeks that she had mentioned my sister.

"She is safe," Father answered. "I believe she is safe."

Without food, but still not hungry, I made my way to the office. There on Mengele's desk stood the two flacons. I could not look in that direction when he came in and called me. "What's the matter, Roman?" he asked, sensing something. For a while now he had addressed me by my first name. Apart from my father, I had become his favourite Gypsy. I told him Zoya was ill. "Don't worry," he said. "I am on the point of conquering the disease. Your wife will recover. Meanwhile you can visit her after your work, and of course you'll see her when I do my rounds. Aren't you pleased?"

"I am," I said.

"I didn't hear you say 'thank you'."

"Thank you, Doctor."

"Good. Now today is an important day. Obersturmbannführer Eichmann from Budapest and Standartenführer Hoess, the camp commandant, are coming to visit the Gypsy camp. This afternoon."

They came. The chain-smoking Hoess, whom I had seen before, and a small man who was the SS Gauleiter of Hungary. He wore breeches, had a cavalryman's gait, and narrow darting eyes. Accompanied by a number of SS officers, including Dr Mengele and Perry Board, they walked around the camp, inspecting the barracks, paying no attention to the Gypsies, almost as if they did not exist. Then they returned to their vehicles and drove off in the direction of the crematoria.

My working time had just finished, so I quickly rushed to the noma barrack, past all the other sick or dying, until I reached Zoya's bunk. She was asleep, breathing heavily, her lids tightened over her eyes with a grimace of suffering. With pain gnawing at my heart, I studied her face. It was already losing its flesh, the open mouth revealing the gums and dark sputum probably by now mixed with yellow pus that I knew was coming from ulcers on the inside of her cheek.

I found Dr Epstein. I did not need to ask him any questions. "She refuses to eat," he said. "We have everything that could help her. Freshly chopped meat, sulphonamides, vitamins. She has lost the will power to stay alive." He put his arm on my shoulder. "Only you can help. I'll have a nurse bring food and medicine. Try to feed her."

I went back and, as soon as a blonde Polish nurse brought a tin plate with meat and vegetables, together with some pills, I woke Zoya up, because I did not know how long I would be allowed to stay with her. Slowly she opened her eyes and looked at me as if in a daze, but this time she did not even utter my name. I tried to spoon some of the meat into her mouth, but she closed it. "Please, Zoya, you must!" A faint flash of recognition passed through her eyes and, miraculously, she unclenched her teeth. I fed her with small spoonfuls of food, then gave her the pills with a glass of water. She had eaten half of the portion given her. "Thank you," I said gratefully, both to her and to God. Exhausted from the effort of eating, she fell asleep.

It was time again for roll-call, so I left the barrack and rejoined my people at the Appellplatz. They began counting us. Then they made us watch Koro Kowal being flogged. He had been working on the building of a railway branch line and had shouted at an SS guard. Those who worked outside Birkenau – and some even did so a few kilometres away in Auschwitz III, run by I. G. Farben, producing rubber – were all brought to the camp for the night.

I told my mother about Zoya starting to eat. My father was not there. I could hear the music of violins. No doubt the German officers, Eichmann, Hoess, Board and Mengele among them, were watching how efficiently the Jewish extermination was taking place to the strains of Gypsy music.

Day after day I managed to visit my wife, and was even encouraged by Mengele to go to her, to feed her and stay with her. But it had nothing to do with any concern for me; he wanted to see a noma patient recover so that he could document the case in his scientific paper on the illness which Dr Epstein called, in Czech, the water cancer. But although she ate, took medicine and even occasionally whispered my name, there was no sign of any improvement. Sometimes I noticed Dr Epstein behind me shake his head and sigh, offering a word or two of encouragement even though I could already see how her left outer cheek was breaking up, perforated and oozing yellow pus.

My mother was hardly able to move after a day of lugging stones. I felt guilty. I should have been doing this work instead of her, but then, if I had, I would not have been able to help, if help it was, my wife in the hospital. My grandfather was sinking. We watched but could do nothing for him, and when he started to talk about food, delicious food, after we got out of Auschwitz, and also time and again pointed at the crematoria, his mood alternating between hope of life and fear of death, we knew that he had already been touched by the angel of death. No longer was he able to wait until he got to an outside latrine; nor could he close his mouth dripping with saliva. His body was all bones; he could not stand upright, only sway, and then began to squat against the wall. All over the camp people were afflicted by this hunger-induced illness, which before Auschwitz had had no name. The Polish doctors called it 'Moslemism', perhaps because of the squatting on the floor. One night my grandfather did not get up from his bunk and my father, who was away with the orchestra, did not even have a chance to kiss him goodbye. He was probably put on to a pyre like the other dying Gypsies, his own son playing the violin as his father's soul left his body that was now charred to ashes.

My father was keeping going as best as he could, even though he had lost both of his parents and daily was witnessing thousands of human beings going into the bath-houses, soap and towel in their hands, and leaving the camp through the chimneys of the crematoria. He had no doubt that, in the end, the same would happen to him and to my mother; but he developed an irrational belief that somehow I would live through it all.

One Sunday after we returned from Lausenkontrolle, the lice control, he took my arm, and led me outside. We walked past my mother who was rubbing clay into her cheeks to try to put some colour into them, past my father-in-law Bora Natkin and my uncle Rudolf Puma trading a Sunday slice of sausage for a bowl of soup, and past the body of Gregory Mular who had died half an hour earlier – with two Gypsies at his bunkside fighting for his underwear, so that they could have double protection against the winter.

My father pointed to the outlines of Birkenau village, which we called Brzezinka and, further on, the church steeple of Auschwitz town, which to us was still Oświęcim. "I am the Shero Rom of our kumpania," he said. "The Shero Rom, with all other eight Council Elders gone. You are not only my son, Roman. You will be the Shero Rom. I want you never to forget what old Szura, who knew our history well, told us around the camp-fire on New Year's Day eighteen months ago. He recalled how almost the entire Gypsy army, which had pursued the Jews fleeing from Egypt, had drowned in the big sea. Now it is happening again. Our nation is sinking. But don't forget what he said then, that a few Gypsies survived and thanks to them our nation was reborn."

He pressed my palms hard with his hands, trying to imbue in me his obstinate desire for me to live, as if it were in my power to decide.

209

My eyes looked obediently towards the outside world, but then they stopped helplessly at the electrified fence around us, interspersed with high watch-towers every hundred metres, where SS men manned searchlights and machine-guns. There was a cattle train halted just behind the camp, for the line now reached Birkenau, to make it easier to discharge the masses of Hungarian Jews who were then marched straight to the crematoria. My father sighed as his eyes turned towards the peaks of the Tatra mountains in the distant south, all his longing for freedom, for travelling and enjoying life mirrored in them. Not for himself, but for me.

"Zoya is in the hospital, and I will not leave her. I won't even try. But if I did, then how?! How am I going to be able to escape?"

"You'll find out how," he said with incredible stubbornness." And then you will let the world know what can't even be imagined. Even if it does learn the truth one day, it will try to forget it as soon as possible. So you must live in order to remind it."

All I could do was to throw my arms around my father. The embrace was a promise, because that was what my father wanted so desperately from me. A promise to fulfil his impossible dream of my escape from Auschwitz.

I was sitting at my table, translating into German a request from a Kelderari woman who was married to a Sinti Wehrmacht veteran, to free her from detention because her husband had earned an Iron Cross on the Russian front. I was to hand the translation to an SS girl typist in my office. But my thoughts were not on the letter. My heart was longing to go as soon as possible to the Nomaabteilung to see my beautiful and lovely Zoya who was no longer beautiful and lovely except in my mind, ravaged as she was by the devastating leprosy-like illness. Dr Mengele was in the adjoining room examining, with the assistance of his Teutonic blonde nurse, a pair of fourteen-year-old twin

210

boys. The door opened and Captain Perry Board entered the barrack and saluted. Mengele immediately left the examining room and returned to his desk, offering his visitor a chair.

"This," Captain Board said, handing him an official-looking envelope with the seal already broken, "has just arrived. From the Reichsführer Heinrich Himmler."

Both men sat down. "Excuse me, Herr Doktor," the nurse said from the other room. "What should I do with those twins?"

"Oh." Mengele raised his head. "I want an autopsy performed on them."

A cold shiver ran through my spine. "Jawohl," the nurse answered, and then ordered an SS guard to take the uncomprehending boys to the barrack where Polish doctors were cutting up bodies and reporting to Dr Mengele on their findings.

Captain Board glanced curiously at the boys as they were being led out, while Mengele pulled out the letter and read it. "I expected this," he said, "shortly after Eichmann's visit. But I did not expect it so soon."

Board spread his fleshy arms. "We have to house them somewhere. Our capacity is 9,000 a day. And they are arriving at a faster rate than that."

I swallowed hard, for though both men probably assumed I could not guess what they were talking about, I remembered the rumour. Half a million Jews from Hungary. Even now, as I looked through the window, I could see the long black serpentine of people on the other side of the barbed wire walking down from the railway track towards the crematoria.

"Tell me," Board asked Mengele. "Why do you have such a great interest in twins? We had 150 pairs of them in BIIF at one time."

"My interest?" Mengele's face became red with excitement. He locked Himmler's letter away in his drawer and pocketed the key, then leaned forward. "Do you know that

I have vivisected six pairs of twins about the same age as those boys and found that the thymus gland, the gland that is so important to the growth of a man and normally becomes smaller and smaller until it practically disappears at the age of puberty, in twins" – he waved his finger – "in twins, and only in twins, it *grows*, becomes larger. Come along later and I'll show you what it is like in those boys."

"And what is the scientific benefit of your discovery?"

Mengele clasped his palms, almost in annoyance. "If we discover all the advantages of being a twin; if in addition we learn how to breed them and at the same time how to improve the human stock – and, believe me, my experiences show that we can lighten the colour of hair and turn brown eyes into blue – we could twice as quickly repopulate those areas emptied of inferior people with the Aryan race. *Twice* as fast, Board!"

The captain nodded. "I'm impressed, Doctor, I'm impressed," he said.

"Unfortunately," Mengele sighed and tapped the drawer in which Himmler's letter was locked, "I may not be allowed to finish my experiments. This Eichmann! Always in such a rush!"

"Space," Board said. "The question of space. Well, I have to go." He got up, clicked his heels and went out.

Mengele slumped back heavily into his chair, burying his head in his hands. Then he took a hold of himself. "We won't do any hospital inspection today," he said.

The nurse returned, followed by the SS guard. "Done as you ordered, Herr Doktor. You want the report today?"

He waved his hand as if he had suddenly lost all his interest. "No, no." He picked up his white gloves and his cavalryman's baton from his desk. "I won't be back today," he told the nurse and the rest of his staff. Soon afterwards I heard his car drive away.

The letter I had translated had been typed long ago; the time dragged. I desperately wanted to see my wife and then run to the camp and warn everyone to prepare for our last stand. Finally the nurse looked at her watch and with Germanic precision said, "In half a minute you can leave." Then she washed her hands, took off her white apron and left, the office staff following her. The SS guards stayed behind, as always.

I ran to the hospital past armed soldiers, orderlies carrying the sick or dead in addition to white-aproned doctors and nurses moving in and out of the barracks – and bolted into the Nomaabteilung, my eyes darting towards Zoya's bunk. My heart froze. It was empty! I dashed forward, frantically searching. She must have been moved to another place. I refused to believe the worst. But I could not find her, methodically though I scanned the room, bunk after bunk, all three tiers.

I rushed over to the wooden partition which was Professor Epstein's cabinet. He was sitting at his desk studying an X-ray against a lamp light. "My wife!" I cried out.

He lowered his eyes. I let out a scream like a wounded animal, then ran all the way back to the bed I had come to twice daily for the past weeks. But no miracle occurred. The bunk was still empty. I slumped down, my fingertips caressing the crumpled blanket left behind. I sat there motionless for a long time, stricken with pain, yet unable to weep and find some relief in tears, for in Auschwitz I had forgotten how to cry. I barely heard the approaching footsteps, the consoling words of Professor Epstein, or his receding steps. Then someone brusquely touched my arm.

"Will you move, please," I heard a Polish nurse say. I turned. Behind her stood two orderlies carrying a stretcher with a new noma patient, a five-year-old boy.

"We need the bed," the nurse said. "And you'd better hurry to the Appellplatz or you'll miss roll-call."

213

5

The bugle call resounded through the camp with a startling shrillness. In the stifling office, where I sat without anything to do, Dr Mengele and a burly SS officer, whom I knew by the name of Friedrich Borger, were discussing the asocial aspect of Gypsies, whom no one, not even the Third Reich, seemed able to tame. There was no question but that they were Aryans, Mengele maintained, as usual wagging his index finger to underline his point, no question about that; and in a hundred years they could even have their physical aspects altered, their hair and skin lightened, their eyes changed to blue – his experiments had shown this to be completely feasible. However, a hundred years was hardly time enough to alter the thousand-year-old habit of never settling down like civilised people.

When the bugle sounded, he glanced at me. "What a pity!" he sighed, as if the bugle had sounded for me. "Let's go." He turned to Borger, grabbing his riding crop. Then he snapped his fingers. "Come with me, Dolmetscher." In front of a stranger he never called me by my first name.

Outside, a group of officers and NCOs awaited Mengele's and Borger's arrival, while armed SS guards and kapos were lining up young Gypsy women along the one side of the Lagerstrasse. A voice from the loudspeaker in one of the watch-towers announced repeatedly that this was a relocation for able-bodied women to help Germany in its war effort and that there was no cause for alarm. Six trucks came into the camp and turned around, their front wheels reassuringly pointed away from the crematoria and towards the camp's exit. The protesting cries ceased and the spirits of the women prisoners rose.

Followed by the others, Dr Mengele started to walk along the line, with a flick of his riding crop directing the women he chose to the other side of the road. When someone strongly objected and he could not understand, he would call to me for help. Any request not to be separated from family was turned down by him as being of no importance, but if a woman was married to a Sinti war veteran he would let her stay.

Slowly he approached to where Sergeant Fürst was busily watching over the women of our barrack, and with a beating heart I saw my mother and next to her my aunt Irina, holding Puji in her arms, as if the baby were a justification for her not to be separated from her husband. My mother's eyes were fixed hopefully on me as if my presence would also protect her. Mengele looked at her, recognised her, did not raise his baton, then my mother said in German pointing at Irina, "My sister." Mengele nodded approval, then went on. I breathed easier; my mother flashed a triumphant and grateful smile to me from the corner of her pale mouth. We were still together, we were still a family.

The selected women were sent back to their barracks to pick up their belongings and return, then they were issued with bread and portions of Cracow sausage, the best there was in Poland, and last distributed in camp on Hitler's birthday. The trucks picked the women up and drove them to a waiting train out of sight. Half an hour later, when the vehicles had made several round trips, we would see the cattle train, its doors open wide, the women waving to us, the sight reassuring to their fathers and husbands who had now hurried towards the barbed wire to wave goodbye to them wherever they were going.

An hour later the bugle call sounded again. I looked, startled, at Dr Mengele. He got up, again as if he were

215

aware of the forthcoming call. "I don't need you, Roman," he said, and left immediately. Through my window I saw once more the same group of officers and NCOs led by Borger, and this time all the young men were being lined up by SS guards and kapos at the side of the road. They were ordered to strip. The routine was repeated: the loudspeaker proclaimed that it was relocation, no cause for alarm, even promising better conditions in another camp. The same six trucks came again. Once more Mengele, riding crop in his hand, walked along the rows of men, selecting the more able-bodied. Those young men, I knew, were the ones who had razors or knives sewn into the lapels of their jackets, but the jackets lay on the ground, my warnings forgotten. Helpless as I was, watching the selection, the fear came over me that perhaps the Nazis were now trying to get rid of any possible resistance and that was why they were picking up men like my uncle Rudolf, and my uncle Leon Kwiatek, and even my father-in-law Bora Natkin, all of whom would turn and fight the SS guards if driven to it. After dressing and picking up their belongings the selected men, now lined up on the other side of the Lagerstrasse, were given bread and Cracow sausage, then driven off. We waited for the train and indeed it soon appeared, the men waving to their families who were allowed to go up to the barbed wire to wave back to them until the train disappeared around a bend.

Mengele returned to his office, accompanied by Borger. "I ordered all those working on the railroad to be transferred to Barrack No. 1, my order effective immediately. We need that second branch line completed as soon as possible. To increase our efficiency."

"Yes," Mengele answered. "Of course."

Some children were waiting in the other room. "Dismiss them," Mengele said to the nurse. "No need."

"I'll see you tonight," Borger said and left.

"Right." Mengele whipped out a typed sheet of paper from his desk drawer, then turned to the nurse again.

216

"Go to the Krankenhaus and take the Dolmetscher with you. I want all the doctors, Polish and Jewish, to sign this, to verify that the camp is infested with typhus, typhoid, dysentery, scarlet fever, etcetera, all highly contagious and dangerous diseases. Make them sign the document."

"Jawohl, Herr Doktor," the woman said, then added, "You remember, you promised me a vacation. A week in Italy starting August 1."

"I remember. Sorry for the delay. But unfortunately Italy is out of the question. Our enemies are pushing hard towards the north. How about Hungary, a lovely resort over Lake Balaton, reserved exclusively for the SS for rest and recuperation?"

The nurse smiled. "Balaton is fine," she said. "I've often heard how beautiful it is."

"Good. You may go on your vacation as of tomorrow. You've worked hard, Schwester. You deserve it."

"The 6 p.m. roll-call has been cancelled," Mengele said, directing everyone in the office to stay on. I felt a heavy weight in my chest. This had never happened before. They brought us food and I partook of it with the office staff and SS guards. Empty cartons were pulled out of a closet. "Pack all the files," Mengele ordered. The nurse, the SS typist and I started on the work.

Darkness fell. Shortly afterwards I could hear the rumble of trucks moving along the Lagerstrasse and halting just opposite us, in front of the Kindergarten. Mengele left the office at once, motioning me to stay behind, and joined the SS officers on the road. A searchlight was focused on the Kindergarten and I could see the silhouettes of helmeted SS guards, rifles in hand, running into the barrack. Shrill, terrified cries of children were heard, followed by heartbreaking pleadings and laments which rose above the noise of running engines. The SS men were dragging boys and girls who called desperately for their parents even though their parents were no longer alive, for all of the children in the Kindergarten were orphans. A few older boys threw themselves on the Nazis, clawing at their faces, but any resistance was immediately quashed by blows from rifle butts which crushed the children's bones. I saw one little boy falling to his knees, clutching Borger's legs with a tearful plea, "Mister SS, please, please have pity on me, let me live!" In response Borger grabbed the child, swung the body and smashed his skull against the truck. Two girls bent down to kiss Mengele's hands, weeping, "Uncle Mengele, Uncle Mengele!" The doctor searched in his pockets and produced, as he always did, a few sweets.

The searchlight was switched off. The hysterical sobbing of the children could be heard from the trucks until the drivers drove off fast towards the crematoria. From afar I could still hear their shrill crying, but then their voices were drowned in the sounds of the orchestra. I knew my father was there, for the first time playing not for the Jews but for the Gypsies, worse, for the Gypsy children, the last sounds of music they were ever to hear.

Mengele returned to the office, glanced at me and then said he was just fulfilling orders. After an hour we heard the trucks again. When they returned empty from the crematoria and stopped in the same place as before, the SS guards this time ran into the Krankenhaus. The entire supervising contingent of SS officers and NCOs led by Borger remained outside on the Lagerstrasse. No one entered our office. Mengele posted an armed guard at the door to prevent any intrusion while we continued to pack the files.

Barrack by barrack, the hospital was being emptied. No one bothered to carry the sick on stretchers. They were pushed by soldiers or, if unable to walk, dragged to the trucks and flung on to them like sacks. Some died on the way, and the dead were thrown in with the living. Then the trucks drove at full speed to the crematoria, discharged their load and returned empty for another until the entire hospital and all its divisions – typhus, typhoid, noma, dysentery, tuberculosis, scarlet fever – had been cleared. In the light that illuminated the hospital area I could see Professor Epstein in his white coat looking for Dr Mengele so that he could appeal to him, but he was stopped by Borger who shouted, "Rauf auf dem Wagen! Get into the truck!"

"Ich bin Jude," Epstein replied.

"Ach so, dann hast du noch ein paar Wochen Zeit. Zurück in die Baracke! As you are a Jew, you still have a few weeks' time. Back into the barrack!" He refused to allow the professor to speak to the chief doctor of the hospital.

The lights were finally switched off as the last trucks left – all the sick had been taken for the last bath at the crematorium. I felt no pain, nor could I cry any more – for how much more can you suffer after your beloved wife has died and most of your people have been taken to be gassed and then burned? Mechanically, like a robot, I completed the packing of the medical files. One truck returned and picked up all the medical personnel from the hospital and drove the doctors and nurses away to Auschwitz I.

Mengele came back. He glanced at his watch. "Almost midnight," he said. Then he looked at the only Gypsy left in the area. I held my breath. "As you can see, I no longer need a Dolmetscher," he added. He beckoned to an SS guard, then out of his pocket he pulled a typewritten sheet and handed it to the soldier. "Take this Gypsy to Barrack No. 1," he said. "It's a transfer to the railway building squad."

I sighed deeply. It could not have been a sigh of relief, for my mind was blank. "Can I get my belongings?" This might be the last chance to see my mother, I thought. On Borger's orders the people working on the Birkenau railway were not allowed back to their barracks.

"No, you can't!" Mengele answered brusquely. "Take him away."

As I walked along the dark Lagerstrasse among the barrack huts where there was still life but without any sight or sound of it, the hushed silence only broken by my footsteps and those of the SS guard, I could not help thinking that the Nazis had found a way of eradicating the spreading epidemics. Simply to gas all the sick and burn their bodies.

From Barrack No.1, the doors to which were guarded by SS men so that no one could venture out, I could see the continuous flames rising from Crematoria No. 1 and No. 2 into the sky and listened to the violins playing Gypsy melodies, the sound of music loud in the quiet night. I wondered what my father was feeling, or whether perhaps, like me, he was feeling nothing at all, his eyes dry, his heart void. In my dark barrack there was one Gypsy from my kumpania, Koro Kowal. But I could not see him. There was a bunk for me, but I did not lie down. As I waited I could tell from the dark outlines of the other prisoners sitting on their bunks or gathering at the windows, that they were waiting too. Once again we heard motor vehicles, as a group of empty trucks returned to the camp, halting at the far end. Reinforcements had been brought in from the outside, machine-gun posts had been set up on the road, and the SS men, with shepherd dogs on leash, moved forwards, to the area where the operation was starting. This time, with the young people removed, the SS men and their kapo henchmen went from barrack to barrack rounding up the Gypsies, not expecting any opposition. But there was furious resistance. I heard sounds of terror, the screams of sobbing children trying to reach their fathers for protection, the women's shrieks of 'Mörder!', but also the cries of men, even the old ones, fighting back. From the dark camp came the vicious howling of dogs, gunshots and bursts of machine-gun fire, as those who threw themselves on the Nazis with knives, razors, sticks or their own bare hands, were selling their lives dearly.

Trucks with their human load rushed to the busy cremaโ toria, then returned empty. Methodically, the vehicles and the SS guards moved down the Lagerstrasse, clearing barrack after barrack. I still could not see them, only heard the sounds of panic and struggle, and I could only imagine how my mother, her sister and little Puji were being pushed and cudgelled on to the trucks.

The operation lasted for several hours, because the Germans were short of transport. Only six trucks were being used. I could now see them, headlights shining as they moved on and stopped, coming nearer and nearer to us, the last barrack on the far side of the main street from the crematoria.

Then suddenly I saw the SS men and their dogs turning on their assistants, the Gypsy kapos who had been helping them to round up their own people. The kapos themselves, protesting in the name of their long service to the Third Reich, were at gunpoint now being forced on to the trucks. Finally only Barrack No. 1 was left. Just one squad of young workers who were still needed to speed up the proโ cess of dispatching to their death the incoming mass of Jews. The camp had become dark, deserted and silent, except for the distant sound of violin music, the clattering of barrack windows and doors left ajar, and the sinister hum of the electrified barbed wire.

Then I heard horses galloping. It was Mengele, in long riding boots, breeches and white gloves, on his regular night ride through the camp. A white stallion also loomed out of the darkness, its rider joining him. It was Hoess, the commandant himself. The two officers halted on the road to look back at the now empty camp. Mengele pointed with his riding crop at the empty barracks. "Schade um die Romantik des Zigeunerlager," he said. "What a pity we have lost the romance of the Gypsy camp." Then he spurred his horse, Hoess following him, and the two officers rode away out of the Zigeunerlager where family life had existed for the past sixteen months until it was snuffed out during the night of August 1, 1944, the night of the Auschwitz massacre of 4,000 Gypsies.

Hours later I was still glued to the window, never having closed my eyes, listening to the orchestra, knowing that my father's music had accompanied my mother on her last journey, yet assured that, as long as I could hear the sounds of his violin, he at least was still alive.

In the first pale light of the breaking day, I saw SS men fanning through the camp, seeking out the few people still hiding in latrines or clinging to roofs, and shooting them on the spot. Then the guns fell silent, the soldiers left, and complete quiet enveloped the camp. Tongues of flame were still rising into the sky from the crematoria, but not a sound was breaking the stillness of the fading night. My hands grabbed at the window-sill. There was no music any more. The violins had stopped playing.

I screamed, for I knew at that moment from the depth of my soul that I would never see my father again. It was the orchestra's turn to take the bath.

6

We were felling trees in the forest that stretched as far as the Sola River and the marshes of the Vistula. A cattle train had just pulled in, a hundred yards from us, to the Birkenau ramp where machine-guns were in position to cover both the incoming Jews and the Gypsy workers. The SS men hurriedly began to unload the trucks, form a line of men, women and children, bundles and battered valises in their hands, and then march them straight towards the Birkenau crematoria.

My group consisted of about twenty men, Koro Kowal among them. Another group was hewing timber into railway sleepers and laying them at intervals on the slightly elevated rail, while a third was carrying steel rails and, under the supervision of German technicians, fastening them to the sleepers and joining them together. It was our job to add the branch line in order to speed up the transport of Jews. We had, I figured, a few weeks' more time, just like Professor Epstein and his colleagues, before our work was completed. I thought wryly how even a criminal like Mengele had had a soft spot in his heart and let me live a bit longer.

We broke for lunch, settling down on the piled-up timbers, with a bowl of soup with a single cabbage leaf and a slice of potato and sawdust bread in our hands. On the ramp stood a new train and a long line of Jews was moving into our camp. The crematoria were overloaded. On the sides of the trucks brief farewell messages to the living had been scribbled almost illegibly in charcoal or blood by those condemned to die.

When, after fifteen minutes, I and my partners picked up our saw again, a sudden thought crossed my mind. If our entire band of young Gypsies, armed with saws and axes, threw themselves on the SS guarding us, we could kill several of them and perhaps some of us would succeed in escaping. If a bullet cut me down – I shrugged at the thought – I would suffer a fate no worse than the rest of my family. Nor would I care, since there was no one left to live for.

But then, almost instantaneously, it dawned on me that I was wrong. I was not alone. There was Mara. Possibly she was safe in the forest farm, some ten or fifteen kilometres away. The image of my little sister – desperately clinging to my father's neck as he tried to push her out of the cattle train – came back to me. All I had to do to find her was follow the railway track south. I felt a pang in my heart, a twinge of emotion, as if I were suddenly coming back to life.

At the end of our work each day we were driven back to our barrack, the only Gypsies in what was now a Jewish camp. One thought had haunted me all afternoon, and was becoming an obsession. Escape, that was what my father had told me. Escape and tell the world. But it was more than that now – escape, find your little sister and live. "You'll be the Shero Rom when I am gone." My father's words resounded in my ears. "Father's words – God's words," my grandfather used to say, as usual quoting a Gypsy proverb to underline the wisdom of his pronouncement. Back in the barrack I began to work out a plan.

My eyes looked over each bunk. The men were eating their evening meal, picking out lice, or chatting among themselves. I did not know them, I could not trust them. The idea of a mass break would never work because someone would betray us, someone who would naïvely hope that denouncing the others might gain him life. And yet it was better for at least two men to run away, so that one could help the other if the need arose. I knew only one man in the barrack. He sat there, not far from me, on his bunk, and I looked at him. Since our fight in the Polish forest eighteen months ago, in Hungary and in the Birkenau camp Koro Kowal and I had not spoken to each other. True, he used to be my rival and I had taken Zoya from him, but Zoya was no longer alive. He was no longer my enemy. He was simply the last Gypsy except me left alive from my kumpania. I got up and walked over to him. "Koro," I said without hesitation, "I am planning to escape. Do you want to escape with me?"

He looked up surprised, baffled, his eyes measuring me. I swallowed hard, because all he had to do to get his revenge was to walk over to an SS guard and report what I had said. His hand rubbed his face as if he were awaking from a bad dream. "Where to?" he uttered.

I lowered my voice. "To that farm where we left my sister. Perhaps we can find shelter there as well."

"We'll never get there. They will shoot us down."

"It's a chance we have to take. We are in the forest already. The trees will offer us some cover and it's easier to disappear in a forest. At least we can give it a try. If not, so what, it's the same end for us as for the others in the squad, only a few weeks earlier."

Koro stared at the floor in front of him. "When do you want to go?"

"Tomorrow. Right after the noon break."

Without looking up at me, he nodded. "Tomorrow then."

"Good night, Koro."

"Good night . . . Roman."

The sun was high above us. My heart pounded as I sat on the slope of the railbed wiping my plate clean with my last piece of bread. I looked over at the guards. They were still eating, heartily – sauerkraut with Cracow sausage and lard with huge chunks of bread; they always got much more than we did and lingered a bit longer to finish their food. Koro, sitting a few metres away from me, and I exchanged

225

glances. An SS sergeant blew a whistle. "Back to work!" he yelled, and we started returning to the forest. One of the soldiers pulled a flask out of his trouser pocket, took a gulp and passed the flask on to a comrade. "Schnaps," he said.

As we had arranged Koro picked up the other end of my saw. I told our previous partners that the change had been ordered by the SS guards. The men knew I spoke German, and they believed me. As I looked back again, I could see that a machine-gun, posted right on the top of the railbed, some fifty metres away, was not manned, and that the SS gunner was still washing his mess tin. There was no time to lose.

"Now!" I said to Koro. "Not together. We must run apart!" And I dashed forward into the forest. Trees rushed by us. Behind me I could hear shouts of 'Verfluchte Banditen!' and rifle shots ricochetting from the tree trunks or whistling by my head. Then the rat-tat-tat of machine-gun fire cracked through the air. But both Koro and I were already in the dense part of the forest where no trees had been felled, where there were no large open spaces, just thick woodland to protect us. The German curses and the bursts of machine-gun fire were fading away behind us. The SS soldiers were burdened by their rifles, we were not.

"Koro!" I shouted.

He was not far from me and he answered. We ran, about fifty metres apart, always towards the south, keeping among the trees, for perhaps a quarter of an hour, perhaps longer, until, completely out of breath, we reached a small clearing. Only now, in the distance, could I hear the sirens sounding the alarm in the camp. The pursuing Nazis would soon be reinforced by a squad of armed men, no doubt accompanied by dogs.

Koro, on the other side of the clearing, was sprawled on the ground, completely out of breath. "We must go on!" I cried, but as I managed to stagger to my feet, an SS man appeared. He emerged from the trees nearby, but he did not notice me. He saw Koro and aimed his gun at him. I threw myself on the man; the bullet grazed my arm, but it did not hit Koro. The German fell to the ground and I found myself, with a strength I did not know I still possessed, on top of him. Desperately I wrestled the gun away from him, smashed the butt down on his head, and then jumped up and shot him. He gasped, a red trickle of blood oozing from his mouth. At that very moment I heard a rustling movement behind me and saw another armed soldier raising his rifle. I fired swiftly before he shot at me. The man staggered, then fell. Koro ran towards him, but there was no need to fight. The soldier was dead, gaping into the sky as if still wondering how it had all happened.

"Get his rifle and ammunition! Quick!" I shouted to Koro. I did not have to repeat my orders. At last, I grinned, I am the Shero Rom of my kumpania, as my father had wished. Or, what was left of my kumpania – Koro and me.

We grabbed all the ammunition which the Nazis had been carrying and, with the rifles in our hands, dashed back into the forest, running and running until I could see, between the dark tree trunks and glistening green foliage, a narrow winding river and beyond it the railway. "There!" I cried. "Look!" We were, no doubt, beyond the main Auschwitz ramp.

Koro's words came between his gasps for air. I knew it was hard for him to say it, but he said it. "Thank you."

I shrugged. It was not Koro's life that I had managed to save, it was another Gypsy's life. My father would have done the same.

From time to time we stopped, but barely for a minute, just to wipe off sweat, to catch our breath, and then continue. I smiled to myself as I had a vision of the hounds losing our tracks as soon as they reached the rippling waters of the River Sola.

We kept forging ahead, guided by the railway track. Suddenly the sound of a locomotive whistle reached my ears, followed by a growing rumble of trucks. "Down!" I snapped. Koro and I flattened ourselves on the forest bed.

I saw a cattle train with armed guards settled on the roofs or running boards between the trucks, all its doors locked and sealed, and signs in charcoal, 'Juden! Auschwitz!' flashing by.

When the rattle had faded into the distance, we got up and went on running, glimpsing the railway line between the trees. Finally I halted abruptly, for I had found what I was looking for – the single track branching out into a double one. I recognised the bushes on the other side of the rails and pushed my way through them. In front of me was a small field and behind it a white farm hut gleaming through the trees.

7

I looked around carefully. There was no one in sight, no sound of any approaching train.

I motioned to Koro, and we both ran across the open field among the green vegetable beds until we reached a patch of tall sunflowers close to the forest. From there I could see not only the white walls and the yellow thatched roof of the little farmhouse, but also part of its backyard, with a little chapel, and a cackling brood of chickens. The mooing of a cow came from a shed I could not see. I dashed into the trees and from there saw a little peasant girl, neatly dressed in a red skirt and white blouse, her dark braids tied with ribbon, playing hop-scotch by herself close to the back porch of the farmhouse.

She reached the final square drawn in the earth and turned around. My heart stopped. It was my sister Mara. Tears, suppressed in the months of camp life, welled up into my eyes. I knew then that I had escaped death, killed the German guards, and managed to stay alive just for this one moment. I could contain myself no longer. Mara was alive – alive and safe! I darted through the open gate of the wooden fence off the backyard. Mara looked up at me, and at Koro right behind me, and, frightened, ran back to the porch, shouting, "Pani Stefa!" I realised then that she had never seen men in strange striped clothes, or holding rifles in their hands.

"Mara! Mara! It's me. Roman!"

The wooden door creaked open and a large peasant woman appeared. She was in her late sixties, dressed in a black robe, her grey hair bound into a severe knot. But my sister was already running towards me. I dropped my rifle, lifted her up into my arms, and covered her little face with kisses. She flung her hands around my neck and burst into uncontrollable sobbing. She recognised Koro and smiled to him. Then she moved her head back. "And Mama and Papa?" she cried out. I answered with a tight hug, and for a moment she forgot her question. She turned to the woman in the doorway. "It's my brother!"

The peasant woman, until now glued to her place, gestured sharply to us. "Get into the house quickly!" she ordered. I picked up my rifle, and we ran into the house. We found ourselves in a kitchen with a large iron stove, pots and strings of onions and garlic hanging on the walls.

"You have escaped from the camp?" the woman asked.

I nodded. She took our rifles from us, opened a latch in the floor close to a wooden sideboard in the corner of the room and threw the rifles down into the cellar.

"Are you being followed?"

"No, no!" I said. "We left the guards behind us long ago."

But the woman dashed into her living room and peered through the window out into the field. She came back to the kitchen, still looking worried. "I can't take any risks," she said, and lifted the cellar door again. "I have this little girl to think about. Go down and wait until I call you."

"Roman!" Mara exclaimed. "You are wounded!"

Only now did I remember the struggle with the German soldier. I looked at my torn sleeve and saw the caked blood on my elbow which his bullet had grazed. "Oh, it's not important."

Quickly and efficiently the peasant woman dipped a tin cup into a water bucket, washed my elbow, then tore a piece of clean kitchen cloth and tied it around my wound. She pushed me forward. "Now, go down, quick."

A rough wooden ladder led down into the cellar. Koro

went first. As I started to descend, Mara ran towards me. "And Mama and Papa?" she asked. "They couldn't get out of that camp?"

"No, darling," I answered. "They could not."

The cellar was dark and cold. With my hands I felt the walls, the shelves, the cans and wooden crates holding potatoes, onions and beets. There were some sacks in one corner and, as I dipped my fingers in, I felt softness and guessed it was flour. Koro said, "Here, we can sit here." I followed his voice. He took my hand and guided me. It was a stack of wooden logs. Above my head I heard what sounded like a heavy piece of furniture, no doubt the sideboard, being dragged over to cover the latch door.

I lapsed into slumber, but constantly jolted awake. Koro's head slumped heavily on to my shoulder. We must have dozed on and off in a restless upright sleep for hours, exhausted by our ordeal. At first I thought I was having a nightmare when I heard the stamping of boots and a gruff German voice asking, "Haben Sie nicht Zwei Flüchtlinge von Kamp gesehen? Have you not seen two escapees from the camp?" The sweat of panic rolled down my forehead. Koro and I groped for our rifles.

"Nein," the woman answered and continued in German, "When did it happen?" In this part of Poland everyone spoke German.

"Today. They killed two of our men. Verfluchte Zigeuner!" Heavy footfalls moving back and forth told us they were searching the house. Then I heard again from the kitchen. "Dieses kleine Mädchen. Wer ist sie?"

"Meine Enkelkind. My granddaughter."

"If you see them," the German continued, "inform the nearest police post immediately. Is there one nearby?"

"Yes, in Potawa, three kilometres away."

"There is a big reward for information leading to their capture. Two thousand marks."

231

I had not seen Mrs Stefa smile, but I was sure that she did so now as she replied, "I wish I had seen them. I could use the money."

"Gut. Heil Hitler!"

"Grüss Gott!"

In the distance I heard a vehicle start, then the noise slowly faded away. We sat on the stack of logs, rifles back on the floor, for at least another hour before I heard the sound of the sideboard moving above us. A streak of light fell upon us, and I could see first the halo of light from a kerosene lamp, then behind it the Polish woman's face. "You can come up," she said.

We scrambled up the ladder. It was evening now, and all the windows were dark. The woman hung her lamp on the nail. "The Germans were here," she said.

"Yes, we could hear them."

"They came on a railway trolley, then left."

"Thank you, Pani Stefa. Thank you very much."

"It was as much my life as yours."

My little sister was standing by the iron stove on which was a large container of boiling water and a big pot of soup which she stirred with a wooden ladle. The kitchen was warm and filled with the aroma of potatoes, carrots and celery roots. "I'm making soup for you," Mara said with a happy twinkle in her eyes.

Through the other open stove rings the firelight was reflected on the white ceiling, making constantly moving shapes. An empty basin, with a coarse piece of washing soap, was on a stool and a bucket of water on the floor. Two worn work suits lay on a chair with high-collared shirts, underwear and socks, and two huge pairs of shoes under the chair. "They belonged to my husband . . . Change quickly and call me when you're ready. But you'd better wash first. We don't want any diseases coming in with you."

She walked to a cabinet and took out a small paper bag containing grey powder. "Do you have lice?"

232

"No," Koro said. "We were disinfected every week in the camp."

"Never mind. Put this on your hair and rub it well in. Come, Mara."

When Koro and I were alone, I poured first hot then cold water into the basin, took off my jacket and undershirt and washed, then threw the dirty water through the side balustrade of the back porch, against the wall of the cowshed. Then Koro washed. We rubbed our hair with the powder, changed into new clothes and slipped our feet into the enormous shoes. "We are ready!" I called.

Pani Stefa returned, followed by Mara. She picked up my camp uniform cautiously with a stick, and pushed it into the stove. She then shoved Koro's clothes into another ring. The fire sizzled. Heavy smoke came out, exuding the stench of burning cotton and sweat. She then repeated the procedure with our shoes. With satisfaction she examined us in our new attire. "My husband was shot five years ago," she said. "By the Germans. They won't come back, certainly not tonight. We shall eat together. But first . . ." She went to the living room and returned with a black kerchief, wrapping it around her head on her way to the door. "Come with me. You, too, Mara."

The woman led us through the courtyard lit only by stars and the dim light of the kerosene lamp in the kitchen. We reached the little chapel with a picture of the Black Madonna framed by red climbing roses. "Let us all pray," the woman said. "And ask for Her protection. For all of us." The woman offered her prayers to the Holy Virgin. With my eyes closed I was repeating her words with all my heart. My arm was around my sister and her head was nestling lovingly and confidently against me.

When we returned to the hut, Pani Stefa closed the shutters, lit another kerosene lamp standing on the table of the living room, and then brought plates, spoons and a loaf of black peasant bread. We began to eat the delicious thick barley and vegetable soup, whole potatoes floating in it, the

233

kind of food that only the SS guards in our camp had enjoyed. The woman smiled as Koro and I polished off our soup and wiped our plates clean with the bread. She poured us second helpings.

"My husband," the woman started to speak, "was a forester, a good forester. With his pay and this small field we were able to support ourselves. Without him I had to hire myself out as a charwoman in Potawa. I had no relatives, no friends – who would bother to come this far to visit me? And yet I could not bring myself to leave the house where I had lived for forty years. So day after day I walked to Potawa, worked hard, returned home at night, with nothing to live for, nobody to live for."

The woman swallowed the tears that came with the memory of her loneliness, but then, as her eyes fell on Mara, her face blossomed into a warm smile. "When that little girl, your sister, ran to me, wrapped her arms around my legs, weeping for her lost family and asking me to take care of her, I felt as if God Himself had sent me this child. I suddenly found a reason to live – to save her."

She leaned forward and brushed her pale wilted lips tenderly against Mara's hair. "People rarely pass by here, and when they do, they pay no attention to the girl. If asked, I tell them it's my granddaughter, whose parents have died. So she doesn't have to hide. But with you it's different. You'll have to stay in the cellar and only come out occasionally when it's dark."

"Thank you, Pani Stefa," I said. "Thank you for Mara, for my friend and myself."

The woman got up, and out of a cupboard pulled a bottle of home-made vodka and three glasses, and filled them up. "Na zdrowie!" She toasted and we all downed our drinks in one gulp, the way Poles do.

"Now I have three reasons to live," the woman continued. A blessed smile lit up her face. She clasped her hands, raised her eyes heavenwards and uttered words I shall never forget. "Thank you, God," she said, "for

234

sending these poor people to me, and giving me the chance of saving them."

Stefa Zlotowska made our shelter as comfortable as she could. She set up a folding canvas cot and hung up a hammock, and supplied us with blankets and pillows. She also gave us a kerosene lamp to be used sparingly and carefully; and Mara brought us potatoes, bread and milk down to the cellar. Whatever the woman had – and she did not have much – she shared with us. The sideboard covered the latch door. Occasionally I heard voices of strangers upstairs, but always Polish – passing railwaymen or peasants who had dropped by for a drink of water or to ask directions.

Stefa Zlotowska did fulfil one feverish wish I had. She went to Potawa and brought back two large notebooks and pencils. In the dim light of the kerosene lamp I wrote. I had plenty of time on my hands. I went back to the day I first learned about Gypsies being taken to the Warsaw ghetto and we had decided to escape. I followed the events with as much detail as I was able, recollecting what happened and even what the people had told me at the time. It was as fresh in my mind as if it were yesterday. And yet in some ways it seemed to be ages ago, at another time, and in another place. I kept my promise to my father.

The summer passed into autumn. The sour smell of hay and dried cow manure penetrated into the cellar through the cracks of the kitchen floor. We kept track of time by listening to the comings and goings of the old woman to milk her cow, which to us were the sunrise and sunset of each separate day. We could tell Sundays by her letting us up at night, leading us to say Paternosters and Ave Marias in the chapel and then allowing us to sit for half an hour together with her and Mara to eat a festive meal of soup and potatoes flavoured with lard.

There was a regular sound every day which we got used to – the rattle of passing trains – and we realised that the

235

Jewish transportations to Auschwitz were still going on. But one day we heard nothing. No clatter of rails, no sounds of engines reached us. The next day, and the day after, there was also uninterrupted silence. The transportations to Auschwitz had ceased. The woman did not let us up, however, because there were truckloads of German troops constantly passing on the road nearby.

The nights grew colder. The last wheat and vegetables had been harvested before the winter came with its frost and strong winds covering the field, the house, the cowshed, and the forest with a blanket of snow. It was cold, very cold, but I kept on writing, filling the pages of my notebooks with the description of events in Poland and Hungary, and in Auschwitz. The weather froze us to the bone, but Koro and I kept a bit warmer by huddling together under our two blankets.

One day we heard the throbbing noise of motor vehicles approaching the house. Koro and I looked at each other fearfully. We heard voices – but they were Russian voices! Not Pani Stefa and Mara, but two soldiers now pushed away the sideboard. "Come up!" one of them called, a boy in Red Army uniform with just a hint of a moustache over his upper lip. "You are free!" Koro and I clambered up the ladder. We embraced the two men. Through the window we saw their armoured car with a Red Star on its front. "The Germans have run away!" the other soldier, a bit older and a corporal, said.

Mara and I, Koro and Pani Stefa fell into each other's arms. Then several Russian soldiers entered the house, bringing with them vodka, sausages and tins of sardines, and Pani Stefa, with Mara's help, cooked a festive meal to celebrate our survival.

"Na zdarowie!" The Russian soldiers raised their glasses and we all drank. We downed not just one, but at least three glasses. A bit tipsy, Koro, my former enemy and now my best friend, looked at my sister now growing up fast, nicely dressed and with her hair beautifully combed with a blue ribbon in her braid. An admiring gleam came into his eyes. He was beginning to take notice of girls, and, once again, of life.

"You may stay here as long as you wish," Stefa Zlotowska said to us.

"We will rest a bit, upstairs if you will permit us," I answered. "But then we ought to move on."

I saw a sorrowful dejected look suddenly cloud the woman's face as she looked at Mara, knowing she could not hold her back. It was as if her life was coming to an end.

"But if you want us to stay with you, we shall for a little while," I added quickly. "We could help you with the crops. We have learned how to fell trees and saw them into logs. We could work hard and support us all."

"Really?" Pani Stefa clasped her hands, then emotionally she threw her arms around Mara. "Stay then! As long as you like."

The Russians rose from their chairs. "The war has ended for you," the corporal said. "But for us we must go on. On to Berlin!"

We waved goodbye to them as their armoured car pulled away across the field and then followed a side path that led to the road.

That day was January 18, 1945, the day I was certain that, no matter how many Gypsies had died in camps or been shot on the roads, the Gypsy nation had survived.